THE SELECTED POEMS OF
ROBERT BURNS

The Selected Poems of

ROBERT BURNS

Edited with an Introduction by
DAVID DAICHES

André Deutsch

First published 1979 by
André Deutsch Limited
105 Great Russell Street London WC1

Copyright © 1979 by David Daiches

Printed in Great Britain by
Clarke, Doble and Brendon Ltd
Plymouth and London

ISBN 0 233 96951 9

CONTENTS

SONGS

INTRODUCTION

Robert Burns is the national poet of Scotland in a way that no other poet is the national poet of his country. Every year on his birthday Scotsmen all over the world gather together for a ritual celebration in which his memory is toasted, his poems recited and his songs sung, and a great deal of whisky is consumed. It is not any great military hero or liberator who is thus celebrated – not William Wallace or Robert the Bruce – but a *poet*. Further, this poet is celebrated as a national hero mostly by people who do not usually read poetry. How can we account for Burns's unique appeal?

The explanation is partly social. Burns was born in humble circumstances, in a clay cottage that his father had built with his own hands in the village of Alloway, two and a half miles south of Ayr. From these humble beginnings he achieved great public acclaim as a poet, admired both by the genteel arbiters of literary taste in Edinburgh and the simple country folk of his own class. This did not bring him money or security, and his short life of thirty-seven years was one of constant strain. But it did mean that a local boy had made good: the son of a gardener who was soon to become a tenant farmer had shown the world what a Scottish peasant from Ayrshire could do. That is one reason perhaps for the fascination he exerts. A more important reason, however, lies in the kind of poetry he wrote.

He was born in "a blast o' Janwar win' " on 25 January 1759. Six years later his father William Burnes (he always spelt his surname with an 'e') leased the farm of Mount Oliphant, a few miles east of Alloway – seventy acres of ill-drained ground at an inflated rent. These were hard times for Ayrshire farmers: farming methods were in transition from the old "run-rig" system to enclosed open farmland with improved drainage, but the heavy clay soil of many Ayrshire farms was still largely undrained at this time, and large rents were exacted in the expectation of improvements that had not yet taken place. If Burns's father had not turned from gardening to farming, Burns later wrote, "I must have marched off to be one of the little underlings about a farm-house: but it was his dearest wish and prayer to have it in his

7

power to keep his children under his own eye till they could discern between good and evil." In 1777 he moved to the 130-acre farm of Lochlie, ten miles to the north-east, for which he paid an even more inflated rent. It was his struggle to keep the farm of Lochlie going under the most difficult circumstances that led to his death, worn out and bankrupt, in 1784.

William Burnes was ambitious for his children, of whom Robert was the eldest. It was not a worldly ambition, but a cultural and educational one. Like so many Scottish peasants of his day, he believed passionately in education as well as in religion, and made every effort to see that his children received proper instruction. When Robert was in his sixth year and the family was still at Alloway, he was sent to a school at Alloway Miln, about a mile away. But the teacher there soon got another job and left, and William Burnes joined with neighbouring farming families in jointly hiring as teacher to their children a rather formal and priggish young man called John Murdoch. Robert and his younger brother Gilbert were given a thorough grounding in English. They progressed rapidly in reading and writing and (as Murdoch later remembered) in "dividing words into syllables by rule, spelling without book, parsing sentences, &c." Murdoch went on to make sure that his pupils read and understood Shakespeare, Milton, Dryden, Pope and other major English writers of the seventeenth and eighteenth centuries. The anthology he used, Arthur Masson's *Collection of Prose and Verse*, included only English literature and as well as extracts from the writers just mentioned had extracts from eighteenth-century poets including Gray, Thomson and Shenstone.

It may seem strange that these rustic young Scots, who spoke a broad Ayrshire Scots among themselves, should have been formally educated wholly in the English language and in English literature. But by Burns's day education in Scotland had long been oriented towards England, and though spoken Scots still flourished among all classes, it was widely believed that this was a corrupt dialect of English (as the great Scottish philosopher David Hume thought) and even distinguished Scottish men of letters had their manuscripts checked by English friends for the removal of "Scotticisms". In earlier times Scots had been a great literary language as well as a vigorous spoken language. The great mediaeval Scottish poets, William Dunbar, Robert Henryson and others, had used a rich and resonant Scots which, while resting on the spoken language, reached out to include all kinds of verbal inventiveness and rhetorical ornamentation. But after the Reformation, which brought the Scots into closer touch with England and brought the English translations of the Bible (first the Geneva Bible of 1560, then the Authorized Version of 1611) to Scottish homes and churches; and after James VI of Scotland moved south with his Court and his Court poets on inheriting the throne of England in 1603; and after the "incorporating union" of 1707 when Scotland lost its separate political identity to become a part of Great Britain ("North Britain" as so many of the eighteenth-century Edinburgh gentry preferred to call it); after all this, Scots as the literary language of Scotsmen who sought reputation and wide readership gave way more and more to standard English. The result was that Scots ceased to be a full-blooded literary language capable of any range of expression and degenerated into a series of regional dialects, used in literature for the most part only by antiquarian imitators, patronizing celebrators of rustic life, naturalistic painters of low life in the city, and parodists. Any ambitious and serious Scottish writer would now use English, the language he was taught at school, as young Burns was taught. His English prose was based on formal eighteenth-century models, and we see it in his letters, accurate, slightly rhetorical, and possessing a studied elegance.

Life at Mount Oliphant was hard. As Gilbert Burns later recalled: "All members of the family exerted themselves to the utmost of their strength, and rather beyond it, in the labours of the farm." Robert at an early age took a principal part in threshing and ploughing, and it was a combination of excessive physical labour and insufficiently nutritious food in youth that produced the first symptoms of that rheumatic heart disease which plagued him for much of his life and from which he eventually died. But somehow he managed to keep reading. Though Murdoch left in 1772 to take up a teaching position at Ayr, Robert was sent to board with him there for a few weeks in 1773 to revise his grammar and to begin the study of French. He was soon summoned back to work on the farm, where he read *Salmon's Geographical Grammar*, and two popular text-books of science which presented scientific facts as evidence of the ingenuity and benevolence of the Creator. He also read a history of Biblical times, and an uncle brought back from a shopping expedition a collection of letters "by the Wits of Queen Anne's reign", which Robert devoured. He discovered the eighteenth-century novel – Richardson's *Pamela*, Fielding's *Tom Jones*, the works of Smollett; he read too the historical works of David Hume and William Robertson. He devoured everything he could lay hands on, begging and borrowing where he could.

Robert later recalled what happened in the latter years at Mount Oliphant. "My father's generous Master died; the farm proved a ruinous bargain; and, to clench the curse, we fell into the hands of a Factor who sat for a picture I have drawn of one in my Tale of two dogs. – My father was advanced in life when he married; I was the eldest of seven children; and he, worn out by early hardship, was unfit for labour . . . We lived very poorly; I was a dextrous Ploughman for my years; and the next eldest to me was a brother, who could drive the plough very well and help me to thrash. – A Novel-Writer might perhaps have viewed these scenes with some satisfaction, but so did not I: my indignation yet boils at the recollection of the scoundrel tyrant's insolent, threatening epistles, which used to set us all in tears." Such a situation nourished Burns's proud egalitarianism, which remained one of the strongest features of his character all his life. He was enraged at the thought that some youngster he had played with as a boy would, because he was the son of a landowner and not of a tenant, in later life give himself airs and require to be deferred to. The rage was even fiercer when the boy in question had no special qualities of mind and character to recommend him. Later he would express with passion his contempt for fools whose only claim to respect lay in their wealth or their title.

In the midst of these troubles, William Burnes was still thinking of his children's education, and in the summer of 1775 sent Robert south-west to the town of Kirkoswald to "a noted school, to learn Mensuration, Surveying and Dialling, &c. in which I made a pretty good progress". He returned home rather more sophisticated than he had come; having fallen passionately in love with one Peggy Thompson and learned, too, something of tavern life. He also enlarged his reading. In this new mood of sophistication he attended a country dancing school "to give my manners a brush," as he later reported, "in absolute defiance" of his father's command. He was becoming something of a rebel and a swaggerer.

The family moved to Lochlie in 1777, and for four years things went fairly well. Then, in Robert's words, "a lawsuit between him and his Landlord commencing, after three years tossing and whirling in the vortex of Litigation, my father was just saved from absorption in a jail by phthisical consumption, which after two years promises, kindly stept in and snatch'd him away – 'To where the wicked cease troubling, and where the weary be at rest'."

During the first four years at Lochlie – probably the happiest ever spent by the Burns family as a whole – Robert made friends at the nearby village of Tarbolton and with some of these he founded the Tarbolton Bachelors' Club in 1780. Here they met every fourth Monday to debate questions that reflected the social problems and ambitions of the members. "Suppose a young man, bred a farmer, but without any fortune, has it in his power to marry any of two women, the one a girl of large fortune, but neither handsome in person nor agreeable in Conversation, but who can manage the household affairs of a farm well enough; the other of them a girl every way agreeable, in person, conversation, and behaviour, but without any fortune: which of them shall he choose?" This was the topic for debate at the first meeting, and it is not hard to guess who chose it. Robert was always falling in love with one girl or another. One of his friends later recalled that "he wore the only tied hair in the parish" and sported an unusually coloured plaid that "he wrapped in a peculiar manner around his shoulders". He was a bit of a show-off, a rebel, restless under the social limitations within which he lived.

In the summer of 1781, anxious to improve the farming prospects at Lochlie, Burns went to Irvine, a flourishing seaport north of Ayr and a centre of the flax-dressing industry; he thought he would learn flax dressing and that he and Gilbert could use part of the farm for the cultivation of flax. But the flax-dresser with whom he entered into partnership proved to be a swindler, and after a fire at a New Year's Eve party in which Burns lost all the possessions he had brought with him he returned to Lochlie frustrated and depressed. Though he had not learned much about flax at Irvine, he had learned something more of the world, and he had met there an educated young seaman called Richard Brown who suggested that the poems Burns had been writing for his own amusement might be worth publishing.

In April 1783 Burns started what he called a Commonplace Book which clearly indicated his interests, his ambitions and his self-consciousness. It began: "Observations, Hints, Songs, Scraps

of Poetry &c. by Robt. Burns; a man who had little art in making
money, and still less in keeping it; but was, however, a man of
some sense, a great deal of honesty, and unbounded good-will
to every creature rational or irrational." He is modelling himself
on the ideal of the "Man of Feeling", the title of a sentimental
novel by the Scottish novelist Henry Mackenzie which Burns
read with eagerness and professed to prize "next to the Bible".
And though he had already written some love songs, partly in
the folk idiom and partly modelled on English verses he had read,
he did not think of himself at this time as a future great poet. But
the tone of the Commonplace Book, and its self-consciously
elegant English style, suggests that he expected that one day it
would be read by posterity.

The death of his father in February 1784 left Burns free to
choose his own kind of life, but it also gave him new responsi-
bilities as head of the family. He and Gilbert managed to extricate
themselves from the consequences of their father's bankruptcy
and, with the help of Gavin Hamilton, a liberal-minded Mauch-
line solicitor, to lease from Hamilton the farm of Mossgiel, only a
few miles from Lochlie in the adjoining parish of Mauchline.
Hamilton was himself a rebel against the narrow orthodoxy of
rural Calvinism, and was in sympathy with the young rebel
farmer. So now Burns was "Rab Mossgiel", known in the
countryside for his liveliness, swagger, rebellious attitude towards
authority and talent for writing verses. These verses were not
only simple love songs. Stimulated by Hamilton's approval and
the friendship of a number of lively Mauchline characters, he
began to write satires on local church affairs, laughing at the
narrowness of the orthodox and the paradoxes invclved in the
conflicting claims of the flesh and religious fervour. He had an
affair with a farm servant Elizabeth Paton and fathered his first
illegitimate child, which he welcomed with a triumphantly
swaggering poem in an old Scottish stanza.

In 1785 he met Jean Armour, daughter of a master mason of
Mauchline, and soon fell in love with her. She became pregnant,
and Burns regarded himself as committed to marriage to her,
as Jean did to him, but Jean's father would not allow his daughter
to marry a known rake and rebel and persuaded Jean to re-
pudiate the mutual contract between them. Burns, furious and
humiliated, took up with another girl, Mary Campbell, about
whom a great deal of legend has grown up but about whom very

little is known, except that she died some months afterwards and
Burns felt wretched and remorseful. He was in deep trouble. The
Kirk was after him for his sexual misdemeanours; Mr Armour
was threatening him with the law to obtain money for the support
of the child that Jean was carrying and Burns feared that he
might be thrown into prison. In desperation he thought of
emigrating to Jamaica. But if he left Scotland, he wanted to
leave behind something by which his country would remember
him. The latter half of 1785 and the first half of 1786 were a
period of brilliant and prolific poetic output, and he now arranged
for John Wilson of Kilmarnock to print an edition of his poems,
which duly appeared on 31 July 1786. *Poems, Chiefly in the Scottish
Dialect*, by Robert Burns, was an overwhelming success, and its
publication radically changed the course of Burns's life.

What sort of poems were these? And how did it come about
that a young man whose education had been wholly in English
literature, in which he had been so thoroughly drilled by Murdoch
before moving on to explore more of it for himself, should have
written poems "chiefly in the Scottish dialect"? This young
tenant farmer had been reading the 'poetry of Thomas Gray,
James Thomson and William Shenstone – he talks in one of his
letters of "the elegantly melting Gray" – for their tender feeling
and proneness to emotional overflow. That way led a rhetorical
sentimentality, which was indeed the genteel literary fashion of
the day, both in London and in Edinburgh. It represented some-
thing quite alien to his genius, something which came in to
distort his poetry and falsify his vision. Shakespeare, Milton,
Dryden, Pope, had nothing but a healthy influence on him: they
stimulated his awareness of poetic craftsmanship and his under-
standing of the workings of the literary imagination. Shenstone
and Henry Mackenzie did him little but harm, and even Gray
and Collins he read for the wrong reasons.

But Burns had also an informal education. His Scottish literary
heritage he had to discover for himself, from three sources. The
first source was the oral folk tradition, the folk tales and folk
songs he heard from the country people and later found in a
great number of eighteenth-century collections, the most im-
portant of which was that produced in two volumes by David
Herd in 1776. The second was the older Scottish literary tra-
dition produced in the days when the rich literary language of
Scotland had not yet declined under the pressure of standard

English into a series of regional dialects. Though relatively little of this was available in Burns's day, and none of it in good texts, some he could find in the selections from older Scottish poetry that were produced throughout the century, by James Watson, Allan Ramsay and others. The third source was the Scots poems of Robert Fergusson, the brilliant young Edinburgh poet who had died in the public bedlam of that city in 1774 at the age of twenty-four. Fergusson showed him a modern Scottish poet using a Scots idiom with artfulness and a keen relish for the colour and variety of the Edinburgh life he knew, and moved him to emulation by applying the same artfulness and satiric vigour in rendering the life of his native Ayrshire. It is the combination of the emotional integrity of the folk tradition, the literary richness and maturity of the "art" tradition of older Scottish literature (even if this only reached him in fragments) and the lessons of craftsmanship that he drew from classical English literature, that is working in Burns's greatest poetry.

The success of the Kilmarnock edition led him to Edinburgh, where he hoped to publish a second edition. There he was befriended, patronized, and showered with well-meant but for the most part impossibly wrong advice. In his preface to the Kilmarnock poems he had deliberately posed as an unlettered peasant, so that the Edinburgh "literati" (as they liked to call themselves) hailed him as, in Henry Mackenzie's words, a "Heaven-taught ploughman". As we have seen, he in fact was remarkably well-read and, as his Commonplace Book and his letters show, he was a conscious poetic craftsman. The "literati" liked his sentimental and rhetorical poems, and encouraged him to write in that vein. Fortunately, he kept his head amid all the patronage and advice, and only rarely succumbed to the style he could do so easily but which did not represent his true genius. His pride and touchiness did him a service here. He knew perfectly well that when he was trotted round the Edinburgh drawing-rooms he was being exhibited as a nine-days' wonder, and that he could not count on his Edinburgh reception to launch him on a fully committed career as the kind of Scottish poet he wanted to be. In fact, the "literati" thought that a Heaven-taught ploughman should go back to the plough, and warble his native wood-notes wild in an appropriate rustic environment. Burns wanted a position in the Excise service. He knew all too well the difficulties and strains of farming in Ayrshire at this time, and wanted a job that would give him some financial security while leaving him free to write his poetry.

Burns sometimes indulged the sentimental–rhetorical side of his nature, encouraged in this as he was by the Edinburgh critics. His duty poem to Edinburgh, beginning with the awful line "Edina! Scotia's darling seat!" is one example of this. But in his great satires, in his artfully woven verse letters, and in his re-creating of almost the whole body of Scottish folk-song (a task which occupied his last years) he drew on the most fruitful part of his reading and listening and on the real strength of his own genius. The difference between the two Burnses can be seen if we compare "To a Mouse", which is an excellent poem, quizzical, half-humorous, cunningly wrought, deftly moving from sudden compassion for the unwittingly deprived little creature to a restrained yet powerful suggestion of his own troubles, with "To a Mountain Daisy", with its whipped up emotion and sentimental posturing. Or we can compare the pompous artificiality of the introductory stanza of "The Cotter's Saturday Night" with the admirable second stanza, setting the scene with a fine handling of weighted language and an artful use of images both particularizing and suggestive. (Here, in fact, he is remembering Gray's "Elegy", but this time to good effect.)

What the Edinburgh "literati" did not see was that Burns operated with his fullest strength and art in his satirical poems. Some of the greatest of these, notably "Holy Willie's Prayer", Burns omitted from the Kilmarnock edition, as he did not want to shock the critics. But even in such a slight poem as "To a Louse" he shows remarkable skill, gently modulating the proud lady to the simple country girl, counterpointing appearance and reality in a context of familiar and fully known and rendered country living. The use of the simple country name "Jenny" to strip the girl of the pretensions which her fine new Lunardi bonnet (called after a balloonist of that name) had produced in her and to restore her, as it were, to common humanity, is art of a high kind. In some degree all Burns's satirical poems deal with appearance and reality, and the ironic gusto, the relish of humanity caught in the act, with which Burns in "The Holy Fair" explores and exposes the truth about human behaviour in a great open-air "tent-preaching" represents something that had not been seen in Scottish poetry since William Dunbar.

In "Holy Willie's Prayer" the use of the dramatic monologue

to reveal unconsciously the full moral horror of the creed in which the speaker devoutly believes, and which he is genuinely professing, is masterly. What we think we are and what we really are – what things are said or claimed to be and what they are in fact – these are the underlying themes in Burns's satires. It is this impulse to restore everything to life, and not to let life be obscured or falsified or sugared over by hypocrisies or artificial distinctions or dead conventions, that we find in so much of Burns's greatest poetry. It is this that leads him to take biblical figures and treat them with a human familiarity that makes them at once more real and closer to ourselves. What other poet could have called the Garden of Eden "Eden's bonnie yaird", or treated Adam and Eve in the Garden as a pair of hapless lovers, or reduced the Devil himself to understandable and familiar proportions?

The Kilmarnock volume also shows Burns as a practitioner of a traditionally Scottish, and very difficult, verse-form – the verse letter. In the best of these he reveals great skill in weaving together the formal and the colloquial, in building a structure that moves easily from the poet's environment to the poet himself, thence to his correspondent, thence to some general ideas, then back again to his correspondent and then signing off. He generally begins by setting the scene and the season, and then, having given the reader the very smell and feel of the poet's time and place, the camera moves, as it were, to the poet writing, and we see him sitting at his desk; thence he moves in an easy and metrically-prepared transition to some general ideas about men and their doings, which in turn generally leads to a climax, a profession of faith, a statement of his position; and then the poem is turned neatly back to poet and correspondent and the conclusion. In some of these verse letters he uses with great adroitness and complexity an old and difficult Scottish stanza.

Edinburgh unsettled Burns. He did not now know quite where he belonged. Lionized though he was, his social position was uncertain; he resented being condescended to by rich and powerful people whom he considered inferior to himself in intelligence. Indeed, Burns arrived in Edinburgh between two phases of Edinburgh's Golden Age. The first had ended with the death of David Hume in 1776, and the second would be the age of Scott and Jeffrey at the beginning of the nineteenth century. In 1786–7 there was no great genius active in Edinburgh and

Burns met few whom he could really consider his intellectual equals. But in April 1786 – the year in which a second, enlarged, edition of his poems was published at Edinburgh – he met James Johnson, a humble, self-educated lover of Scottish song who had invented a cheap process for printing music by using stamped pewter plates and proposed to publish a "Collection of Scots, English and Irish Songs". The first volume was already in the press when Johnson asked Burns for help in collecting Scottish songs for subsequent volumes. Burns responded with enormous enthusiasm, and soon he had virtually taken over the direction of the work, *The Scots Musical Museum*: between early 1787 and late 1792 the bulk of Burns's production was songs for Johnson. In 1792 he was approached by the more genteel George Thomson for similar help in his collection of *Select Scottish Airs*, and again Burns responded enthusiastically.

By this time Burns's life had become very complicated. In May 1787 he had made a tour of the Border country. In June he returned to Mauchline to be welcomed as a hero. Jean Armour's parents now thought that this man who had been feted by the great of Edinburgh was eminently suitable as a husband for their daughter; but their fawning disgusted him, and though he took up with Jean again (and she became pregnant again) he did not contemplate marriage. He returned to Edinburgh in August, and set out from there for a three weeks' tour of the Highlands during which he familiarized himself with local folk songs and got the "feel" of different parts of Scotland. He made a tour in Stirlingshire in October, then returned to Edinburgh, restless and undecided about his future. There he conducted a strangely hot-house love affair with Mrs Agnes M'Lehose, an attractive young woman deserted by her rascally husband; they exchanged highly rhetorical letters and he wrote her some poems, of which the finest is the one he wrote when they parted, "Ae fond kiss, and then we sever".

In March 1788 Burns finally acknowledged Jean Armour as his wife (in Scots law he was able to do this retroactively in virtue of their former association) and in June, somewhat against his better judgement, he settled on the farm of Ellisland (six and a half miles north-west of Dumfries) that had been offered to him on lease by Patrick Miller, an Edinburgh banker who admired his poetry. The land was, as Miller later admitted, "in the most miserable state of exhaustion" and proved impossible to work profitably. Burns had been taking a course of instruction in Excise matters and finally in September 1789, after many pressing applications on his part, he got an appointment in the "Dumfries first Itinerary". At first he combined his Excise duties (which involved watching for smuggling and seeing that weights and measures conformed to the legal standard) with farming, but this proved altogether too exhausting and on 10 September 1791, with the greatest relief, Burns signed a formal renunciation of the Ellisland lease and in the following November moved to Dumfries, where he lived until his death on 21 July 1796.

Burns's last years vividly illustrated the paradoxical nature of his social position. He was invited to the homes of the surrounding landed gentry, notably the family of Robert Riddell who lived on the Glenriddell estate at Friars' Carse less than a mile north of Ellisland. He was entertained, patronized and befriended, because of his genius. His wife had no share in these visits or entertainments, being a simple Scots lass of no great education and totally unable to play any part in the witty social conversation at which Burns shone. Thus his social relationships were wholly separated from his domestic life and were sometimes dangerously balanced between equality and (on his hosts' part) condescension. Burns had already learned that the witty and polished daughters of the gentry would happily chat with him but would take alarm at once if Burns ventured any suggestion of social and sexual equality. He was thus torn between girls he admired socially and girls who accepted his sexual love. Jean, who loved him in spite of his periodic bouts of unfaithfulness, and whom he loved in spite of everything, accepted him for what he was. But Robert suffered alternating moods of high passion and deep depression, exasperatedly conscious of his precarious balance between two worlds. He got himself into political trouble by showing sympathy with the French Revolution after it broke out: Burns's fierce egalitarianism, so proudly asserted in "A man's a man for a' that", responded generously to this movement, and he was encouraged in this attitude by Dr William Maxwell, a new friend he made in Dumfries (one of several) who had travelled in France and come back ardent in support of the Revolution. He made his peace with the authorities when he turned against the Revolution after its excesses and especially by the patriotic sentiments voiced in poems after Britain went to war with France; he joined the Dumfries Volunteers in January 1795. By this time he was a very sick man, afflicted with recurring bouts of rheumatic fever. He was sent to Brow on the Solway Firth in July 1796 in the preposterous belief that sea-bathing might cure him. He returned to his house in Dumfries on the 16th and died there on the 21st.

In his latter years Burns's poetic activity was largely taken up with songs for Johnson and Thomson: he continued working on these until within a few days of his death. He refused to take money for this work, considering it his patriotic duty to collect, preserve and re-create the songs of Scotland. The only other significant new variety of poetry he produced during his Dumfriesshire period was the remarkable narrative poem "Tam o' Shanter", written at the end of 1790. In its handling of the octosyllabic couplet, in its movement and variation of pace, in its use of Scots and introduction of formal English in ironic moral sentimentalizing (in the passage beginning "But pleasures are like poppies spread"), in its effective contrast between the cosy interior of the pub and the dark and stormy night outside, in the adroit combination of humour, sympathy, horror, irony and reproof, this poem showed what Burns could have done in this genre if he had lived. But it remains an isolated example.

As for his songs, written often in an English tipped with Scots, sometimes in a Scots tipped with English, showing at their best a delicate ability to combine elements from English and Scots speech and a remarkable gift for setting words to existing tunes – these remain perhaps his greatest popular legacy throughout the world. He took the crumbling and half-forgotten fragments of his country's folk songs and restored them sometimes by complete re-writing, sometimes by supplying new verses to an old chorus, sometimes by filling out a mere suggestion he found in some half-remembered line or barely surviving chorus. He undertook to find words – old or refurbished or new – to all the existing Scottish airs that he thought worth preserving, whether they existed in the eighteenth century as song tunes or as dance tunes. It is important to remember that these are songs, written to specific airs, and that without these airs they lose a dimension.

Burns picked up work songs from fisher folk on the Moray Firth or the Fife coast, or from farmers in his native Ayrshire, or from anywhere that he wandered in his journeyings around Scotland, and gave them new form and new life. Always in his songs he is concerned with the cycle of life and love and work as he knew it. An unpretentious fisher song from Fife, "Hey, Ca'

Thro' ", is as significant to him as a gentle love song such as "Afton Water". Many songs he never claimed as his ("Auld Lang Syne", for example) but simply sent to Johnson or Thomson as an old song he had discovered. But we can recognize Burns's hand by the way he manages to capture the moment of realized passion, the timeless emotion when the whole of experience is centred on what is happening here and now, with a lyrical intensity which is all the stronger because of the simplicity of the expression. "My luve is like a red, red rose" (a re-working of old material) has that combination of tenderness and swagger, of protectiveness and bravado, that is so characteristic of the male in love. But he could sing the songs of the other sex too, and some of his finest love songs are put in the mouths of girls. He linked love, sex and parenthood in a way that no other poet has done: he rejoiced in all three. He saw these things as they were and at his best expressed them with moving clarity. In a sense, he was not a romantic but an unromantic. He never wrote of the magnificent mountains and the sounding sea, but of the trotting or toddling burn, the braeside, the girl by his side on a country walk, all against a background of seasonal work, man both against nature and with nature. He could celebrate friendship as well as love, drink as well as sex, work as well as play, anger and indignation as well as happiness. He spoke for man's "unofficial self" (to borrow a phrase George Orwell used in another context). Sometimes he expressed a mood of sheer joyous anarchy, as in his "Cantata" entitled "Love and Liberty" (generally known as "The Jolly Beggars").

The pressures on him of the genteel culture of his day sometimes proved irresistible. They drove him on occasion to the grossest sentimentalities or rhetorical posturing. Yet in the main this Ayrshire peasant resisted the advice and criticism of professors and leaders of literary fashion and stuck to what he knew he could do best. It is no service to Burns to wax enthusiastic over his occasional surrender to hypocrisy and gentility. The satirist, the song-writer, the quizzical writer of animal poems, the master of the verse letter, the master (on one great occasion only) of octosyllabic narrative verse, the celebrator of man as he is – that is the Burns who lives. The great annual welling up of feeling about him on his birthday is testimony enough that, for all the flatulent nonsense talked at Burns Suppers, there is a human voice here of a very special kind.

TEXTUAL NOTE

The standard text of Burns's poems is that established by James Kinsley's authoritative edition of the poems in 1968. Professor Kinsley's primary source was Burns's own manuscripts; his other sources were the Kilmarnock edition of 1786, the Edinburgh editions of 1787–94, Johnson's *Scots Musical Museum* and Thomson's *Select Collection of Original Scottish Airs*, transcripts of manuscripts not now accessible and early printings in newspapers, periodicals and chapbooks.

I have not adopted Kinsley's text in this collection, though I have made abundant use of it. In a selection of Burns's poems intended both for schools and for the general reader, the text should surely be easily readable as well as accurate. But accuracy here means something slightly different from the scholarly accuracy of the editor of a definitive text. The scholar will want to reproduce the asterisks, the dashes, the idiosyncratic (and inconsistent) punctuation, the profuse use of italics, and other features of the manuscripts and the early printed texts. He will want to record faithfully every time Burns used the old Scots ending *-an* or *-and* for the present participle *-ing*, and when he used *-in*, as well as when he used *-it*, and when he used *-et* for the past. He will faithfully print "Oh" where Burns has "Oh" and "O" where Burns has "O", even though it is clear that Burns used the two forms indifferently and inconsistently.

The text of this selection of poems, then, is accurate in the sense that nowhere does it do violence to what Burns wrote, though it may sometimes alter his punctuation and occasionally alter a spelling. I see no point in preserving the anonymity of characters referred to in certain poems by reproducing the asterisks of the Kilmarnock edition. I have not followed Burns's (or his early printers') use of italics. I have even, occasionally – where Burns himself produced several different versions, each of which he claimed to be the best – produced a slightly eclectic text, as in "Auld Lang Syne", where no line occurs that is not recorded by Burns as accurate, but where I have tried also to take notice of those readings which have become traditional through generations of singing. (Thus I have not printed "For all lang syne, my jo" but adopted the regularly sung "For auld lang syne, my dear", which is also a Burns version but does not occur in the particular copy he wrote out in which all the other features of the text I use occur.) I have kept Burns's use of the *–an* participle ending in most cases where Burns himself used it, but as he himself was thoroughly inconsistent in his usage I have allowed myself to be so also.

In the songs, I have printed the chorus first and, to remind the readers that they are indeed *songs*, I have added the name of the tune for which Burns wrote them except in those cases where the name of the tune is identical with the title of Burns's song.

As for the order of the poems, I have set them out in what is likely to have been their order of composition within each category. In the case of posthumously published songs, as indeed in other cases too, this order cannot always be definitely established. I have in fact followed Kinsley's order, except that each category is ordered independently.

D.D.

Satires

ADDRESS TO THE UNCO
GUID

OR THE RIGIDLY RIGHTEOUS

My Son, these maxims make a rule,
An' lump them ay thegither:
The Rigid Righteous is a fool,
The Rigid Wise anither;
The cleanest corn that e'er was dight   sifted
May hae some pyles o' caff in;   chaff
So ne'er a fellow-creature slight
For random fits o' daffin.   fun
        SOLOMON (*Eccles.* vii. 16)

I

O ye wha are sae guid yoursel,
  Sae pious and sae holy,
Ye've nought to do but mark and tell
  Your neebours' fauts and folly!
Whase life is like a weel-gaun mill,   well-going
  Supplied wi' store o' water;
The heapet happer's ebbing still,   heaped hopper
  An' still the clap plays clatter.   clapper

2

Hear me, ye venerable core,   company
  As counsel for poor mortals
That frequent pass douce Wisdom's door   sober
  For glaikit Folly's portals: giddy
I, for their thoughtless, careless sakes
  Would here propone defences,   propose
Their donsie tricks, their black mistakes,   unlucky
  Their failings and mischances.

3

Ye see your state wi' theirs compared,
    And shudder at the niffer;

difference

But cast a moment's fair regard,
    What makes the mighty differ?
Discount what scant occasion gave,
    That purity ye pride in;

rest

And (what's aft mair than a' the lave)
    Your better art o' hidin.

4

Think, when your castigated pulse
    Gies now and then a wallop,
What ragings must his veins convulse,
    That still eternal gallop:
Wi' wind and tide fair i' your tail,
    Right on ye scud your sea-way;
But in the teeth o' baith to sail,

strange

    It makes an unco lee-way.

5

See Social-life and Glee sit down
    All joyous and unthinking,
Till, quite transmugrify'd, they're grown
    Debauchery and Drinking:
O, would they stay to calculate,
    Th' eternal consequences,
Or, your more dreaded hell to state,
    Damnation of expenses!

6

Ye high, exalted, virtuous dames,
    Tied up in godly laces,
Before ye gie poor Frailty names,
    Suppose a change o' cases:
A dear-lov'd lad, convenience snug,
    A treach'rous inclination –

ear
maybe

But, let me whisper i' your lug,
    Ye're aiblins nae temptation.

7

Then gently scan your brother man,
  Still gentler sister woman;
Tho' they may gang a kennin wrang,
  To step aside is human:
One point must still be greatly dark,
  The moving *why* they do it;
And just as lamely can ye mark
  How far perhaps they rue it.

8

Who made the heart, 'tis He alone
  Decidedly can try us:
He knows each chord its various tone,
  Each spring its various bias:
Then at the balance let's be mute,
  We never can adjust it;
What's *done* we partly may compute,
  But know not what's *resisted*.

HOLY WILLIE'S PRAYER

And send the godly in a pet to pray.
POPE

Argument

Holy Willie was a rather oldish bachelor Elder in the parish of Mauchline, and much and justly famed for that polemical chattering which ends in tippling orthodoxy, and for the spiritualized bawdry which refines to liquorish devotion. In a sessional process with a gentleman of Mauchline, a Mr Gavin Hamilton, Holy Willie, and his priest, Father Auld, after full hearing in the Presbytery of Ayr, came off second best, owing partly to the rhetorical powers of Mr Robt. Aiken, Mr Hamilton's Counsel, but chiefly to Mr Hamilton's being one of the most irreproachable and truly respectable characters in the country. On losing his process, the Muse overheard him in his devotions as follows. [Burns's headnote.]

O Thou that in the Heavens does dwell,
Wha, as it pleases best thysel,
Sends ane to Heaven an' ten to Hell
      A' for thy glory,
And no for onie guid or ill
      They've done before Thee.

I bless and praise thy matchless might,
When thousands thou has left in night,
That I am here before thy sight,
      For gifts an' grace
A burning and a shining light
      To a' this place.

What was I, or my generation,
such   That I should get sic exaltation?
I, wha deserv'd most just damnation
      For broken laws
Six   Sax thousand years ere my creation,
      Thro' Adam's cause!

28

Holy Willie's Prayer

When from my mither's womb I fell,
Thou might hae plung'd me deep in hell
To gnash my gooms, and weep, and wail   gums
                      In burning lakes,
Whare damned devils roar and yell,
                      Chain'd to their stakes.

Yet I am here, a chosen sample,
To show thy grace is great and ample:
I'm here, a pillar o' thy temple,
                      Strong as a rock,
A guide, a buckler, and example
                      To a' thy flock!

But yet, O Lord, confess I must:
At times I'm fash'd wi' fleshly lust;   troubled
An' sometimes, too, in warldly trust,
                      Vile self gets in;
But Thou remembers we are dust,
                      Defil'd wi' sin.

O Lord, yestreen, thou kens, wi' Meg –   last night; knowest
Thy pardon I sincerely beg!
O, may't ne'er be a living plague
                      To my dishonour!
An' I'll ne'er lift a lawless leg
                      Again upon her.

Besides, I farther maun avow –   must
Wi' Leezie's lass, three times, I trow –
But, Lord, that Friday I was fou   drunk
                      When I cam near her,
Or else, thou kens, thy servant true
                      Wad never steer her.   Would; disturb

Maybe thou lets this fleshly thorn
Buffet thy servant e'en and morn,
Lest he owre proud and high should turn   too
                      That he's sae gifted;
If sae, thy han' maun e'en be borne
                      Until thou lift it.

29

Lord, bless thy chosen in this place,
For here thou has a chosen race:
But God, confound their stubborn face
        An' blast their name,
Wha bring thy elders to disgrace
        An' open shame!

Lord, mind Gau'n Hamilton's deserts:

cards — He drinks, an' swears, an' plays at cartes,
Yet has sae monie takin arts
        Wi' great and sma',
Frae God's ain priest the people's hearts
        He steals awa.

And when we chasten'd him therefore,

uproar — Thou kens how he bred sic a splore,
And set the warld in a roar
        O' laughin at us:
Curse thou his basket and his store,

Cabbage —   Kail an' potatoes!

Lord, hear my earnest cry and pray'r
Against that Presbyt'ry of Ayr!
Thy strong right hand, Lord, mak it bare
        Upo' their heads!

do not — Lord, visit them, an' dinna spare,
        For their misdeeds!

O Lord, my God! that glib-tongu'd Aiken!
My vera heart and flesh are quakin
To think how we stood sweatin, shakin,
        An' piss'd wi' dread,

sneering — While he, wi' hingin lip an' sneakin,
        Held up his head.

Lord, in thy day o' vengeance try him!
Lord, visit him wha did employ him!
And pass not in thy mercy by them,
        Nor hear their pray'r,
But for thy people's sake destroy them,
        An' dinna spare!

But, Lord, remember me and mine
Wi' mercies temporal and divine,

wealth — That I for grace an' gear may shine,
        Excell'd by nane;
And a' the glory shall be Thine!
        Amen, Amen!

DEATH AND DOCTOR HORNBOOK

A True Story

Some books are lies frae end to end,
And some great lies were never penn'd:
Ev'n ministers, they hae been kend,
          In holy rapture,
A rousing whid at times to vend,   lie
          And nail't wi' Scripture.

But this that I am gaun to tell,   going
Which lately on a night befel,
Is just as true's the Deil's in hell
          Or Dublin city:
That e'er he nearer comes oursel
          'S a muckle pity!

The clachan yill had made me canty,   village ale; merry
I was na fou, but just had plenty: drunk
I stacher'd whyles, but yet took tent ay staggered now and
          To free the ditches;   then; care; clear
An' hillocks, stanes, an' bushes, kenn'd ay
          Frae ghaists an' witches.

The rising moon began to glowr
The distant Cumnock Hills out-owre: beyond
To count her horns, wi' a' my pow'r
          I set mysel;
But whether she had three or four,
          I cou'd na tell.

I was come round about the hill,
And todlin down on Willie's mill,
Setting my staff wi' a' my skill
          To keep me sicker;   steady
Tho' leeward whyles, against my will,   at times
          I took a bicker.   short rush

31

I there wi' *Something* does forgather,
put; strange flurry That pat me in an eerie swither;
across one An awfu' scythe, out-owre ae shouther,
　　　　　Clear-dangling, hang;
three-pronged fish-spear A three-tae'd leister on the ither
　　　　　Lay, large an' lang.

Its stature seem'd lang Scotch ells twa,
The queerest shape that e'er I saw,
never a belly; at all For fient a wame it had ava,
　　　　　And then its shanks,
They were as thin, as sharp an' sma'
wooden bridle 　　　　　As cheeks o' branks.

"Guid-een," quo' I; "Friend! hae ye been mawin,
When ither folk are busy sawin?"
halt It seem'd to mak a kind o' stan',
　　　　　But naething spak.
where are ye going At length, says I, "Friend! whare ye gaun?
　　　　　Will ye go back?"

hollow It spak right howe, "My name is Death,
scared But be na' fley'd." Quoth I, "Guid faith,
Ye're may be come to stap my breath;
heed; comrade 　　　　　But tent me, billie:
advise; harm I red ye weel, take care o' skaith,
large knife 　　　　　See, there's a gully!"

knife "Gudeman," quo' he, "put up your whittle,
I'm no design'd to try its mettle;
likely to be mischievous But if I did, I wad be kittle
　　　　　To be mislear'd:
I wad na mind it, no that spittle
　　　　　Out-owre my beard."

"Weel, weel!" says I, "a bargain be't;
give us; agreed Come, gie's your hand, an' say we're gree't;
We'll ease our shanks an' tak a seat:
　　　　　Come, gie's your news:
road This while ye hae been monie a gate,
　　　　　At monie a house."

"Ay, ay!" quo' he, an' shook his head,
"It's e'en a lang, lang time indeed
Sin' I began to nick the thread   cut
               An' choke the breath:
Folk maun do something for their bread,   must
               An' sae maun Death.

"Sax thousand years are near-hand fled   well-nigh
Sin' I was to the butching bred,   butchering
An' monie a scheme in vain's been laid
               To stap or scar me;   stop; scare
Till ane Hornbook's ta'en up the trade,
               And faith! he'll waur me.   worst

"Ye ken Jock Hornbook i' the clachan?   village
Deil mak his king's-hood in a spleuchan!   scrotum; tobacco-
He's grown sae weel acquaint wi' *Buchan**   pouch
               And ither chaps,
The weans haud out their fingers laughin,   children
               An' pouk my hips.   poke; buttocks

"See, here's a scythe, an' there's a dart,
They hae pierc'd monie a gallant heart;
But Doctor Hornbook wi' his art
               An' cursèd skill,
Has made them baith no worth a fart,
               Damn'd haet they'll kill!   The devil a one

" 'Twas but yestreen, nae farther gane,   gone
I threw a noble throw at ane;
Wi' less, I'm sure, I've hundreds slain;
               But deil-ma-care!
It just played dirl on the bane,   went tinkle
               But did nae mair.

"Hornbook was by wi' ready art,
An' had sae fortify'd the part,
That when I looked to my dart,
               It was sae blunt,
Fient haet o't wad hae pierc'd the heart
               Of a kail-runt.   cabbage-stalk

* A medical textbook: William Buchan's *Domestic Medicine*.

"I drew my scythe in sic a fury,

tumbled
I near-hand cowpit wi' my hurry,
But yet the bauld Apothecary
　　　　　　Withstood the shock:
I might as weel hae try'd a quarry
　　　　　　O' hard whin-rock.

"Ev'n them he canna get attended,
Altho' their face he ne'er had kend it,
Just shit in a kail-blade an' send it,
　　　　　　As soon's he smells 't,
Baith their disease and what will mend it,
　　　　　　At once he tells 't.

"And then a' doctor's saws and whittles
Of a' dimensions, shapes, an' mettles,
A' kinds o' boxes, mugs, and bottles,
　　　　　　He's sure to hae;
Their Latin names as fast he rattles
　　　　　　As A B C.

"Calces o' fossils, earth, and trees;
True *sal-marinum* o' the seas;
The *farina* of beans an' pease,
　　　　　　He has't in plenty;
Aqua fontis, what you please,
　　　　　　He can content ye.

"Forbye some new, uncommon weapons,
Urinus spiritus of capons;
Or mite-horn shavings, filings, scrapings,
　　　　　　Distill'd *per se*;
Sal-alkali o' midge-tail clippings,
　　　　　　And monie mae."

"Waes me for Johnie Ged's* Hole now,"
Quoth I, "if that thae news be true!
His braw calf-ward whare gowans grew
　　　　　　Sae white and bonie,
Nae doubt they'll rive it wi' the plew:
　　　　　　They'll ruin Johnie!"

* The grave-digger.

34

The creature grain'd an eldritch laugh   groaned; ghastly
And says: "Ye nedna yoke the pleugh,
Kirkyards will soon be till'd eneugh,
         Tak ye nae fear:
They'll a' be trench'd wi monie a sheugh   ditch
         In twa-three year.

"Whare I kill'd ane, a fair strae-death   straw, i.e. bed
By loss o' blood or want o' breath,
This night I'm free to tak my aith,
         That Hornbook's skill
Has clad a score i' their last claith   cloth
         By drap an' pill.

"An honest wabster to his trade,   weaver
Whase wife's twa nieves were scarce weel-bred,   fists
Gat tippince-worth to mend her head,
         When it was sair;   aching
The wife slade cannie to her bed,   crept quietly
         But ne'er spak mair.

"A countra laird had taen the batts,   botts [colic]
Or some curmurring in his guts,   commotion
His only son for Hornbook sets,
         An' pays him well:
The lad, for twa guid gimmer-pets,   pet-ewes
         Was laird himsel.

"A bonie lass – ye kend her name –
Some ill-brewn drink had hov'd her wame;   put up; belly
She trusts hersel, to hide the shame,
         In Hornbook's care;
Horn sent her aff to her lang hame
         To hide it there.

"That's just a swatch o' Hornbook's way;   sample
Thus goes he on from day to day,
Thus does he poison, kill, an' slay,
         An's weel paid for't;
Yet stops me o' my lawfu' prey
         Wi' his damn'd dirt!

"But, hark! I'll tell you of a plot,
Tho' dinna ye be speakin o't:
I'll nail the self-conceited sot,
                    As dead's a herrin;

next; wager

Niest time we meet, I'll wad a groat,

deserts

                    He gets his fairin!"

But just as he began to tell,
The auld kirk-hammer strak the bell

beyond twelve

Some wee short hour ayont the twal,

got us to our legs

                    Which raised us baith;
I took the way that pleas'd mysel,
                    And sae did Death.

THE HOLY FAIR*

A robe of seeming truth and rust
Hid crafty observation;
And secret hung, with poison'd crust,
The dirk of defamation:
A mask that like the gorget show'd
Dye-varying on the pigeon;
And for a mantle large and broad,
He wrapt him in Religion.

HYPOCRISIE ALAMODE†

I

Upon a simmer Sunday morn,
   When Nature's face is fair,
I walkèd forth to view the corn,
   An' snuff the caller air.   fresh
The rising sun, owre Galston Muirs,
   Wi' glorious light was glintan;   glancing
The hares were hirplan down the furrs,   hopping; furrows
   The lav'rocks they were chantan   larks
             Fu' sweet that day.

2

As lightsomely I glowr'd abroad,   gazed
   To see a scene sae gay,
Three hizzies, early at the road,   young women
   Cam skelpan up the way.   spanking
Twa had manteeles o' dolefu' black,
   But ane wi' lyart lining;   grey
The third, that gaed a wee a-back,   walked a bit behind
   Was in the fashion shining
             Fu' gay that day.

3

The twa appear'd like sisters twin,
   In feature, form, an' claes;   clothes
Their visage wither'd, lang an' thin,
   An' sour as onie slaes: shoes
The third cam up, hap-step-an'-lowp,   hop; jump
   As light as onie lambie,
An' wi' a curchie low did stoop,   curtsey
   As soon as e'er she saw me,
             Fu' kind that day.

* *Holy Fair* is a common phrase in Scotland for a sacramental occasion. [Burns's note.]
† *The Stage Beaux toss'd in a Blanket; or Hypocrisie Alamode*, by Tom Browne, 1704.

4

Wi' bonnet aff, quoth I, "Sweet lass,
   I think ye seem to ken me;
I'm sure I've seen that bonie face,
   But yet I canna name ye."
Quo' she, an' laughan as she spak,
   An' taks me by the han's,

bulk

"Ye, for my sake, hae gi'en the feck
   Of a' the Ten Comman's

rip

         A screed some day.

5

"My name is Fun – your cronie dear,
   The nearest friend ye hae;
An' this is Superstition here,
   An' that's Hypocrisy.

going
frolic

I'm gaun to Mauchline Holy Fair,
   To spend an hour in daffin:

wrinkled

Gin ye'll go there, yon runkl'd pair,
   We will get famous laughin
         At them this day."

6

Quoth I, "Wi' a' my heart, I'll do't;

shirt

   I'll get my Sunday's sark on,
An' meet you on the holy spot;

we'll

   Faith, we'se hae fine remarkin!"

went; breakfast-time

Then I gaed hame at crowdie-time,
   An' soon I made me ready;
For roads were clad, frae side to side,
   Wi' monie a wearie body,
         In droves that day.

7

shrewd; gear
jogging

Here farmers gash, in ridin graith,
   Gaed hoddan by their cotters;

strapping youngsters

There swankies young, in braw braid-claith,
   Are springan owre the gutters.

padding; thronging

The lasses, skelpan barefit, thrang,
   In silks an' scarlets glitter;

slice

Wi' sweet-milk cheese, in monie a whang,

small cakes

   An' farls, bak'd wi' butter,

crisp

         Fu' crump that day.

8

When by the plate we set our nose,
  Weel heapèd up wi' ha'pence,
A greedy glowr Black-bonnet throws,   the Elder
  An' we maun draw our tippence.   must
Then in we go to see the show:
  On ev'ry side they're gath'ran;
Some carryan dails, some chairs an' stools,   planks
  An' some are busy bleth'ran   gabbling
        Right loud that day.

9

Here stands a shed to fend the show'rs,   keep off
  An' screen our countra gentry;
There Racer Jess, an' twa-three whores,   two or three
  Are blinkan at the entry.   leering
Here sits a raw o' tittlan jads,   whispering jades
  Wi' heavin breasts an' bare neck;
An' there a batch o' wabster lads,   weaver
  Blackguarding frae Kilmarnock,
        For fun this day.

10

Here some are thinkan on their sins,
  An' some upo' their claes;
Ane curses feet that fyl'd his shins,   soiled
  Anither sighs an' prays:
On this hand sits a chosen swatch,   sample
  Wi' screw'd-up, grace-proud faces;
On that a set o' chaps, at watch,
  Thrang winkan on the lasses   Busy
        To chairs that day.

11

O happy is that man an' blest!
  Nae wonder that it pride him!
Whase ain dear lass, that he likes best,
  Comes clinkan down beside him!   sitting down
Wi' arm repos'd on the chair back,
  He sweetly does compose him;
Which, by degrees, slips round her neck,
  An's loof upon her bosom,   And his palm
        Unkend that day.

39

12

Now a' the congregation o'er
　　Is silent expectation;
climbs For Moodie* speels the holy door,
　　Wi' tidings o' damnation:
the Devil Should Hornie, as in ancient days,
　　'Mang sons o' God present him;
The vera sight o' Moodie's face
hot 　　To's ain het hame had sent him
　　　　Wi' fright that day.

13

Hear how he clears the points o' Faith
　　Wi' rattlin an' thumpin!
Now meekly calm, now wild in wrath,
　　He's stampan, an' he's jumpan!
His lengthen'd chin, his turn'd-up snout,
ghastly 　　His eldritch squeel an' gestures,
O how they fire the heart devout,
　　Like cantharidian plaisters
　　　　On sic a day!

14

But hark! the tent has chang'd its voice;
There's peace an' rest nae langer;
For a' the real judges rise,
　　They canna sit for anger:
Smith† opens out his cauld harangues,
　　On practice and on morals;
An' aff the godly pour in thrangs,
　　To gie the jars an' barrels
　　　　A lift that day.

15

What signifies his barren shine,
　　Of moral pow'rs an' reason?
His English style, an' gesture fine
　　Are a' clean out o' season.
Like Socrates or Antonine,
　　Or some auld pagan heathen,
The moral man he does define,
　　But ne'er a word o' faith in
　　　　That's right that day.

* The Rev. Alexander Moodie. 　† The Rev. George Smith.

The Holy Fair

16

In guid time comes an antidote
  Against sic poison'd nostrum;
For Peebles,* frae the water-fit,   *river's mouth*
  Ascends the holy rostrum:
See, up he's got the word o' God,
  An' meek an' mim has view'd it,
While Common-sense has taen the road,
  An' aff, an' up the Cowgate
        Fast, fast that day.

17

Wee Miller† niest, the guard relieves,   *next*
  An' orthodoxy raibles,   *gabbles*
Tho' in his heart he weel believes,
  An' thinks it auld wives' fables:
But faith! the birkie wants a manse: *fellow; living*
  So, cannilie he hums them;   *humbugs*
Altho' his carnal wit an' sense
  Like hafflins-wise o'ercomes him   *nearly hal*
        At times that day.

18

Now butt an' ben the change-house fills,   *tavern*
  Wi' yill-caup commentators;   *ale-cup*
Here's crying out for bakes an' gills,   *biscuits*
  An' there the pint-stowp clatters;
While thick an' thrang, an' loud an' lang,
  Wi' logic an' wi' Scripture,
They raise a din, that in the end
  Is like to breed a rupture
        O' wrath that day.

19

Leeze me on drink! it gies us mair   *Blessings*
  Than either school or college;
It kindles wit, it waukens lear,   *learning*
  It pangs us fou o' knowledge: *crams*
Be't whisky-gill or penny wheep,   *small beer*
  Or onie stronger potion,
It never fails, on drinkin deep,
  To kittle up our notion,   *tickle*
        By night or day.

---

* The Rev. William Peebles.   † The Rev. Alexander Miller.

20

The lads an' lasses, blythely bent
    To mind baith saul an' body,
Sit round the table, weel content,
    An' steer about the toddy:
stir
On this ane's dress, an' that ane's leuk,
    They're makin observations;
corner
While some are cozie i' the neuk,
    An' formin assignations
        To meet some day.

21

sounds
But now the Lord's ain trumpet touts,
roaring
    Till a' the hills are rairin,
And echoes back return the shouts;
    Black Russell* is na spairan:
His piercin words, like highlan' swords,
    Divide the joints an' marrow;
His talk o' Hell, whare devils dwell,
    Our vera "sauls does harrow"
        Wi' fright that day.

22

A vast, unbottom'd, boundless pit,
full; flaming
    Fill'd fou o' lowin brunstane,
Whase raging flame, an' scorching heat,
    Wad melt the hardest whun-stane!
The half-asleep start up wi' fear,
    An' think they hear it roaran;
When presently it does appear,
    'Twas but some neebor snoran
        Asleep that day.

23

'Twad be owre lang a tale to tell,
    How monie stories past,
An' how they crouded to the yill,
    When they were a' dismist:
How drink gaed round, in cogs an' caups,
    Amang the furms an' benches;
An' cheese an' bread, frae women's laps,
large slices
    Was dealt about in lunches,
lumps
        An' dawds that day.

* The Rev. John Russell, minister at Kilmarnock, a strict Calvinist much disliked by Burns.

24

In comes a gawsie, gash guidwife,   jolly
 An' sits down by the fire,
Syne draws her kebbuck an' her knife; Then; cheese
 The lasses they are shyer.
The auld guidmen, about the grace,
 Frae side to side they bother,
Till some ane by his bonnet lays,
 An' gies them't, like a tether,   rope
    Fu' lang that day.

25

Waesucks! for him that gets nae lass, Alas!
 Or lasses that hae naething!
Sma' need has he to say a grace,
 Or melvie his braw claithing!   soil with meal
O wives, be mindfu', ance yoursel,
 How bonie lads ye wanted,
An' dinna for a kebbuck-heel
 Let lasses be affronted
    On sic a day!

26

Now Clinkumbell, wi' rattlan tow,   the bell-ringer; rope
 Begins to jow an' croon;   swing and toll
Some swagger hame the best they dow, can
 Some wait the afternoon.
At slaps the billies halt a blink,   openings; fellows; bit
 Till lasses strip their shoon: take off
Wi' faith an' hope, an' love an' drink,
 They're a' in famous tune
    For crack that day.   talk

27

How monie hearts this day converts
 O' sinners and o' lasses!
Their hearts o' stane, gin night, are gane by nightfall; gone
 As saft as onie flesh is:
There's some are fou o' love divine;
 There's some are fou o' brandy;
An' monie jobs that day begin,
 May end in houghmagandie   fornication
    Some ither day.

43

THE TWA DOGS

A Tale

'Twas in that place o' Scotland's isle
That bears the name of auld King Coil,*
Upon a bonie day in June,
When wearing thro' the afternoon,
busy — Twa dogs, that were na thrang at hame,
got together — Forgathered ance upon a time.

The first I'll name, they ca'd him Caesar,
Was keepit for his Honor's pleasure:
ears — His hair, his size, his mouth, his lugs,
Shew'd he was nane o' Scotland's dogs;
But whalpit some place far abroad,
Whare sailors gang to fish for cod.

His lockèd, letter'd, braw brass collar
Shew'd him the gentleman an' scholar;
But tho' he was o' high degree,
The devil a bit of pride — The fient a pride, nae pride had he;
But wad hae spent an hour caressan,
mongrel — Ev'n wi' a tinkler-gipsy's messan;
smithy — At kirk or market, mill or smiddie,
matted cur; ragged — Nae tawted tyke, tho' e'er sae duddie,
would have stood — But he wad stan't, as glad to see him,
pissed — An' stroan't on stanes an' hillocks wi' him.

The tither was a ploughman's collie,
rollicking fellow — A rhyming, ranting, raving billie,
Wha for his friend an' comrade had him,
And in his freaks had Luath ca'd him,
After some dog in Highland sang,†
Was made lang syne – Lord knows how lang.

* Kyle, the middle district of Ayrshire.
† Cuchullin's dog in Ossian's "Fingal". [Burns's note.]

44

The Twa Dogs

He was a gash an' faithfu' tyke,   *wise*
As ever lap a sheugh or dyke.   *ditch; stone fence*
His honest, sonsie, baws'nt face   *pleasant, white-*
Ay gat him friends in ilka place;   *streaked; every*
His breast was white, his touzie back   *shaggy*
Weel clad wi' coat o' glossy black;
His gawsie tail, wi' upward curl,   *joyous*
Hung owre his hurdies wi' a swirl.   *buttocks*

Nae doubt but they were fain o' ither,   *fond of each other*
And unco pack an' thick thegither;   *confidential*
Wi' social nose whyles snuff'd an' snowkit;   *now*
Whyles mice an' moudieworts they howkit;   *moles; dug*
Whyles scour'd awa' in lang excursion,
An' worry'd ither in diversion;
Till tir'd at last wi' monie a farce,
They sat them down upon their arse,
An' there began a lang digression
About the "lords o' the creation."

CAESAR

I've aften wonder'd, honest Luath,
What sort o' life poor dogs like you have;
An' when the gentry's life I saw,
What way poor bodies liv'd ava.   *at all*

Our laird gets in his rackèd rents,
His coals, his kane; an' a' his stents: *rents in kind; dues*
He rises when he likes himsel;
His flunkies answer at the bell;
He ca's his coach; he ca's his horse;
He draws a bonie silken purse,
As lang's my tail, whare, thro' the steeks,   *stitches*
The yellow, letter'd Geordie keeks.   *guinea peeps*

45

Frae morn to e'en it's nought but toilin
At baking, roasting, frying, boiling;
cramming An' tho' the gentry first are stechin,
servants; stomach Yet ev'n the ha' folk fill their peghan
Wi' sauce, ragouts, an sic like trashtrie,
That's little short o' downright wastrie:
Our whipper-in, wee, blastit wonner,
Poor, worthless elf, it eats a dinner,
Better than onie tenant-man
His Honor has in a' the lan';
put; paunch An' what poor cot-folk pit their painch in,
I own it's past my comprehension.

LUATH

sometimes; bothered Trowth, Caesar, whyles they're fash't ene
digging A cotter howkan in a sheugh,
building Wi' dirty stanes biggan a dyke,
clearing Bairan a quarry, an' sic like;
Himsel, a wife, he thus sustains,
litter; ragged kids A smytrie o' wee duddie weans,
hands' labour An' nought but his han'-darg to keep
thatch and rope Them right an' tight in thack an' rape.
An' when they meet wi' sair disasters,
Like loss o' health or want o' masters,
small Ye maist wad think, a wee touch langer,
must An' they maun starve o' cauld and hunger:
But how it comes, I never kent yet,
They're maistly wonderfu' contented;
stout lads; young An' buirdly chiels, an' clever hizzies,
women Are bred in sic a way as this is.

CAESAR

But then to see how ye're negleckit,
How huff'd, an' cuff'd, an' disrespeckit!
Lord man, our gentry care as little
For delvers, ditchers, an' sic cattle;
They gang as saucy by poor folk,
badger As I wad by a stinkan brock.

46

The Twa Dogs

I've notic'd, on our laird's court-day,
(An' monie a time my heart's been wae),   sad
Poor tenant bodies, scant o' cash,
How they maun thole a factor's snash: endure; abuse
He'll stamp an' threaten, curse an' swear,
He'll apprehend them, poind their gear;   seize
While they maun staun', wi' aspect humble,   stand
An' hear it a', an' fear an' tremble!

I see how folk live that hae riches;
But surely poor-folk maun be wretches!

LUATH

They're nae sae wretched's ane wad think:
Tho' constantly on poortith's brink,   poverty's
They're sae accustom'd wi' the sight,
The view o't gies them little fright.

Then chance an' fortune are sae guided,
They're ay in less or mair provided;
An' tho' fatigu'd wi' close employment,
A blink o' rest's a sweet enjoyment.   snatch

The dearest comfort o' their lives,
Their grushie weans an' faithfu' wives;   growing
The prattling things are just their pride,
That sweetens a' their fire-side.

An' whyles twalpennie worth o' nappy   sometimes; ale
Can mak the bodies unco happy:
They lay aside their private cares,
To mind the Kirk an' State affairs;
They'll talk o' patronage an' priests,
Wi' kindling fury i' their breasts,
Or tell what new taxation's comin,
An' ferlie at the folk in Lon'on.   marvel

As bleak-fac'd Hallowmass returns,
They get the jovial, rantan kirns,   harvest-homes
When rural life, of ev'ry station,
Unite in common recreation;
Love blinks, Wit slaps, an' social Mirth   glances
Forgets there's Care upo' the earth.

47

That merry day the year begins,
They bar the door on frosty win's;
foaming froth   The nappy reeks wi' mantling ream,
An' sheds a heart-inspiring steam;
smoking; snuff-box   The luntin pipe, an' sneeshin mill,
Are handed round wi' right guid will:
conversing cheerfully   The cantie auld folks crackan crouse,
romping   The young anes rantan thro' the house –
My heart has been sae fain to see them,
That I for joy hae barkit wi' them.

Still it's owre true that ye hae said
too often   Sic game is now owre aften play'd;
There's monie a creditable stock
respectable   O' decent, honest, fawsont folk,
Are riven out baith root an' branch,
Some rascal's pridefu' greed to quench,
Wha thinks to knit himsel the faster
In favor wi' some gentle master,
maybe busy   Wha, aiblins thrang a parliamentin',
indenturing   For Britain's guid his saul indentin' –

CAESAR

Haith, lad, ye little ken about it:
For Britain's guid! guid faith! I doubt it.
going   Say rather, gaun as Premiers lead him,
An' saying *aye* or *no*'s they bid him:
At operas an' plays parading,
Mortgaging, gambling, masquerading:
Or maybe, in a frolic daft,
To Hague or Calais taks a waft,
To mak a tour an' tak a whirl,
To learn *bon ton*, an' see the worl'.

There, at Vienna or Versailles,
breaks up   He rives his father's auld entails;
road   Or by Madrid he taks the rout,
fight; cattle   To thrum guitars an' fecht wi' nowt;
Or down Italian vista startles,
Whore-hunting amang groves o' myrtles:
muddy   Then bowses drumlie German-water,
To mak himsel look fair an' fatter,
sores   An' purge the bitter ga's an' cankers
venereal sores   O' curst Venetian bores an' chancres.

48

The Twa Dogs

For Britain's guid! for her destruction!
Wi' dissipation, feud an' faction.

LUATH

Hech man! dear sirs! is that the gate   way
They waste sae monie a braw estate!
Are we sae foughten an' harass'd   troubled
For gear ta gang that gate at last?   wealth to go

O would they stay aback frae courts,
An' please themsels wi' countra sports,
It wad for ev'ry ane be better,
The laird, the tenant, an' the cotter!
For thae frank, rantin, ramblin billies,   those; roistering
Fient haet o' them's ill-hearted fellows: Not one
Except for breakin o' their timmer,   wasting their woods
Or speakin lightly o' their limmer,   mistress
Or shootin of a hare or moor-cock,
The ne'er-a-bit they're ill to poor folk.

But will ye tell me, master Caesar:
Sure great folk's life's a life o' pleasure?
Nae cauld nor hunger e'er can steer them,
The vera thought o't need na fear them.   touch

CAESAR

Lord, man, were ye but whyles whare I am,
The gentles, ye wad ne'er envy em!

It's true, they need na starve or sweat,
Thro' winter's cauld, or simmer's heat;
They've nae sair wark to craze their banes,

hard

An' fill auld-age wi' grips an' granes:

gripes and groans

But human bodies are sic fools,
For a' their colleges an' schools,
That when nae *real* ills perplex them,
They *mak* enow themsels to vex them;

fret

An' ay the less they hae to sturt them,
In like proportion, less will hurt them.

A countra fellow at the pleugh,
His acre's till'd, he's right eneugh;
A countra girl at her wheel,

dozen

Her dizzen's done, she's unco weel;
But gentlemen, an' ladies warst,

positive

Wi' ev'n down want o' wark are curst:
They loiter, lounging, lank an' lazy;

nothing

Tho' deil-haet ails them, yet uneasy:
Their days insipid, dull an' tasteless;
Their nights unquiet, lang an' restless.

An' ev'n their sports, their balls an' races,
Their galloping through public places,
There's sic parade, sic pomp an' art,
The joy can scarcely reach the heart.

The men cast out in party-matches,

solder

Then sowther a' in deep debauches;

One

Ae night they're mad wi' drink an' whoring,

Next

Niest day their life is past enduring.

The ladies arm-in-arm in clusters,
As great an' gracious a' as sisters;
But hear their absent thoughts o' ither,

downright

They're a' run deils an' jads thegither.
Whyles, owre the wee bit cup an' platie,
They sip the scandal-potion pretty;

live-long

Or lee-lang nights, wi' crabbit leuks

i.e. playing cards

Pore owre the devil's pictur'd beuks;
Stake on a chance a farmer's stackyard,
An' cheat like onie unhang'd blackguard.

The Twa Dogs

There's some exceptions, man an' woman;
But this is Gentry's life in common.

By this, the sun was out o' sight,
An' darker gloamin brought the night;   twilight
The bum-clock humm'd wi' lazy drone;   beetle
The kye stood rowtin' i' the loan;   cattle; lowing; field
When up they gat, an' shook their lugs,   side path
Rejoic'd they were na *men*, but *dogs*;   ears
An' each took off his several way,
Resolv'd to meet some ither day.

ADDRESS TO THE DEIL

O Prince, O Chief of many thronèd pow'rs,
That led th' embattl'd seraphim to war.

MILTON

Cloven-footed

O Thou! whatever title suit thee –
Auld Hornie, Satan, Nick, or Clootie –
Wha in yon cavern grim an' sootie,
            Clos'd under hatches,

Splashes; dish
scald

Spairges about the brunstane cootie,
              To scaud poor wretches!

Hangman

Hear me, Auld Hangie, for a wee,
An' let poor damnèd bodies be;
I'm sure sma' pleasure it can gie,
            Ev'n to a deil,

spank; scald

To skelp an' scaud poor dogs like me
            An' hear us squeel.

Great is thy pow'r an' great thy fame;
Far kend an' noted is thy name;

flaming hollow

An' tho' yon lowin heugh's thy hame,
            Thou travels far;

backward
bashful; afraid

An' faith! thou's neither lag, nor lame,
            Nor blate, nor scaur.

Now

Whyles, ranging like a roarin lion,
For prey, a' holes an' corners trying;
Whyles, on the strong-wing'd tempest flyin,

Stripping

            Tirlan the kirks;
Whyles, in the human bosom pryin,
            Unseen thou lurks.

I've heard my rev'rend graunie say,
In lanely glens ye like to stray;
Or, where auld ruin'd castles grey
            Nod to the moon,
Ye fright the nightly wand'rer's way

ghastly

            Wi' eldritch croon.

Address to the Deil

When twilight did my graunie summon,
To say her pray'rs, douce, honest woman,   sedate
Aft yont the dyke she's heard you bummin,   beyond
      Wi' eerie drone;
Or, rustlin, thro' the boortrees comin,   alders
      Wi' heavy groan.

Ae dreary, windy, winter night,   One
The stars shot down wi' sklentin light,   squinting
Wi' you, mysel, I gat a fright:
      Ayont the lough,   pond
Ye, like a rash-buss, stood in sight;   clump of rushes
      Wi' waving sugh.   moan

The cudgel in my nieve did shake,   fist
Each bristl'd hair stood like a stake;
When wi' an eldritch, stoor "quaick, quaick,"   harsh
      Amang the springs,
Awa ye squatter'd like a drake,
      On whistling wings.

Let warlocks grim, an' wither'd hags,
Tell how wi' you, on ragweed nags,   ragwort
They skim the muirs an' dizzy crags,
      Wi' wicked speed;
And in kirk-yards renew their leagues,
      Owre howkit dead.   exhumed

Thence, countra wives, wi' toil an' pain,
May plunge an' plunge the kirn in vain;   churn
For Och! the yellow treasure's taen
      By witching skill;
An' dawtit, twal-pint hawkie's gaen   petted, twelve-pint
      As yell's the bill.   cow; gone dry as; bull

Thence, mystic knots mak great abuse
On young guidmen, fond, keen an' croose;   husbands; merry or cocksure; tool
When the best wark-lume i' the house,
      By cantraip wit,   magic
Is instant made no worth a louse,
      Just at the bit.   nick of time

53

thaws; hoard

When thowes dissolve the snawy hoord,
An' float the jinglin icy boord,
Then, water-kelpies haunt the foord,
            By your direction,
An' nighted trav'llers are allur'd
                To their destruction.

bog; will-o'-the-wisps

And aft your moss-traversing spunkies
Decoy the wight that late an' drunk is:
The bleezin, curst, mischievous monkies
            Delude his eyes,
Till in some miry slough he sunk is,
                Ne'er mair to rise.

must

straight

When Masons' mystic word an' grip
In storms an' tempests raise you up,
Some cock or cat your rage maun stop,
            Or, strange to tell!
The youngest brother ye wad whip
                Aff straught to hell.

garden

Lang syne in Eden's bonie yard,
When youthfu' lovers first were pair'd,
An' all the soul of love they shar'd,
            The raptur'd hour
Sweet on the fragrant flow'ry swaird,
                In shady bow'r:

crafty

trick

shake

Then you, ye auld, snick-drawing dog!
Ye cam to Paradise incog,
An' play'd on man a cursèd brogue
            (Black be your fa'!),
An' gied the infant warld a shog,
                'Maist ruin'd a'.

flurry
smoky; scorched wig
smutty

squinted

D'ye mind that day when in a bizz
Wi' reekit duds, an' reestit gizz,
Ye did present your smoutie phiz
            'Mang better folk;
An' sklented on the man of Uzz
                Your spitefu' joke?

54

Address to the Deil

An, how ye gat him i' your thrall,
An' brak him out o' house an' hal',
While scabs an' botches did him gall,   blotches
   Wi' bitter claw;
An' lows'd his ill-tongu'd wicked scaul –   loosed; scold
   Was warst ava?   of all

But a' your doings to rehearse,
Your wily snares an' fechtin fierce,   fighting
Sin' that day Michael did you pierce
   Down to this time,
Wad ding a Lallan tongue, or Erse,   beat; Lowland
   In prose or rhyme.

An' now, Auld Cloots, I ken ye're thinkin,
A certain Bardie's rantin, drinkin,   roistering
Some luckless hour will send him linkin,   hurrying
   To your black Pit;
But, faith! he'll turn a corner jinkin,   dodging
   An' cheat you yet.

But fare-you-weel, Auld Nickie-Ben!
O' wad ye tak a thought an' men'!
Ye aiblins might – I dinna ken –   perhaps
   Still hae a stake:
I'm wae to think upo' yon den,   sad
   Ev'n for your sake!

TO A LOUSE

ON SEEING ONE ON A LADY'S
BONNET AT CHURCH

Ha! whare ye gaun, ye crowlan ferlie?
Your impudence protects you sairly:
I canna say but ye strunt rarely
        Owre gauze and lace,
Tho' faith! I fear ye dine but sparely
        On sic a place.

Ye ugly, creepan, blastit wonner,
Detested, shunn'd by saunt an' sinner,
How daur ye set your fit upon her –
        Sae fine a lady!
Gae somewhere else and seek your dinner
        On some poor body.

foot

Swith! in some beggar's hauffet squattle:
There ye may creep, and sprawl, and sprattle,
Wi' ither kindred, jumping cattle,
        In shoals and nations;
Whare horn nor bane ne'er daur unsettle
        Your thick plantations.

Off!; temples squat
scramble

Now haud you there! ye're out o' sight,
Below the fatt'rils, snug an' tight;
Na, faith ye yet! ye'll no be right,
        Till ye've got on it –
The vera tapmost, tow'ring height
        O' Miss's bonnet.

keep
ribbon ends

My sooth! right bauld ye set your nose out,
As plump an' grey as onie grozet:
O for some rank, mercurial rozet,
        Or fell, red smeddum,
I'd gie ye sic a hearty dose o't,
        Wad dress your droddum!

gooseberry
rosin
deadly; powder

backside

To a Louse

I wad na been surpris'd to spy   would not have
You on an auld wife's flainen toy;   flannel cap
Or aiblins some bit duddie boy,   maybe;
           On's wyliecoat;   small ragged undervest
But Miss's fine Lunardi! fye!   balloon-shaped bonnet
           How daur ye do't?

O Jenny, dinna toss your head,
An' set your beauties a' abread!   abroad
Ye little ken what cursèd speed
           The blastie's makin!
Thae winks an' finger-ends, I dread,   Those
           Are notice takin!

O wad some Power the giftie gie us
To see oursels as others see us!
It wad frae monie a blunder free us,
           An' foolish notion:
What airs in dress an' gait wad lea'e us,
           An' ev'n devotion!

Animal Poems

THE DEATH AND DYING WORDS OF POOR MAILIE

THE AUTHOR'S ONLY PET YOWE: AN UNCO MOURNFU' TALE

As Mailie, an' her lambs thegither,   *Mollie; together*
Was ae day nibbling on the tether,   *one*
Upon her cloot she coost a hitch,   *hoof; looped*
An' owre she warsl'd in the ditch: *floundered*
There, groaning, dying, she did lie,
When Hughoc he cam doytan by.   *doddering*

Wi' glowrin een, an' lifted han's   *staring*
Poor Hughoc like a statue stan's;
He saw her days were near-hand ended,
But, wae's my heart! he could na mend it!   *woe*
He gapèd wide, but naething spak.
At length poor Mailie silence brak:

"O thou, whase lamentable face
Appears to mourn my woefu' case!
My dying words attentive hear,
An' bear them to my Master dear.

"Tell him, if e'er again he keep   *own*
As muckle gear as buy a sheep,   *much money*
O, bid him never tie them mair,
Wi' wicked strings o' hemp or hair!
But ca' them out to park or hill,   *drive*
An' let them wander at their will:
So may his flock increase, an' grow
To scores o' lambs, an' packs o' woo'!

"Tell him, he was a Master kin',
An' ay was guid to me an' mine;
An' now my dying charge I gie him,
My helpless lambs, I trust them wi' him.

61

"O, bid him save their harmless lives,
foxes Frae dogs, an' tods, an' butchers' knives!
But gie them guid cow-milk their fill,
look after Till they be fit to fend themsel;
tend An' tent them duly, e'en an' morn,
small quantities; Wi' teats o' hay an' ripps o' corn.
handfuls

ways "An' may they never learn the gaets
restless Of ither vile, wanrestfu' pets,
breaches To slink thro' slaps, an' reave an' steal,
At stacks o' pease, or stocks o' kail.
So may they, like their great forbears,
For monie a year come thro' the sheers:
So wives will gie them bits o' bread,
weep An' bairns greet for them when they're dead.

tup [ram] "My poor toop-lamb, my son an' heir,
O, bid him breed him up wi' care!
An' if he live to be a beast,
behaviour To pit some havins in his breast!
will not An' warn him – what I winna name –
ewes To stay content wi' yowes at hame;
An' no to rin an' wear his cloots,
unmannerly Like other menseless, graceless brutes.

ewekin; helpless "An' niest, my yowie, silly thing,
Gude keep thee frae a tether string!
make friends O, may thou ne'er forgather up,
Wi' onie blastit, moorland toop;
nibble; meddle But ay keep mind to moop an' mell,
Wi' sheep o' credit like thysel!

"And now, my bairns, wi' my last breath,
I lea'e my blessin wi' you baith:
An' when you think upo' your mither,
Mind to be kind to ane anither.

"Now, honest Hughoc, dinna fail,
To tell my master a' my tale;
An' bid him burn this cursèd tether,
bladder An' for thy pains thou'se get my blether."

This said, poor Mailie turn'd her head,
eyes An' clos'd her een amang the dead!

62

POOR MAILIE'S ELEGY

Lament in rhyme, lament in prose,
Wi' saut tears tricklin down your nose;
Our Bardie's fate is at a close,
        Past a' remead!   remedy
The last, sad cape-stane of his woes;
        Poor Mailie's dead!

It's no the loss of warl's gear,   worldly goods
That could sae bitter draw the tear,
Or mak our Bardie, dowie, wear   sad
        The mourning weed:
He's lost a friend an' neebor dear
        In Mailie dead.

Thro' a' the toun she trotted by him;   farm
A lang half-mile she could descry him;
Wi' kindly bleat, when she did spy him,
        She ran wi' speed:
A friend mair faithfu' ne'er cam nigh him,
        Than Mailie dead.

I wat she was a sheep o' sense,   wot
An' could behave hersel wi' mense: tact
I'll say 't, she never brak a fence,
        Thro' thievish greed.
Our Bardie, lanely, keeps the spence   parlour
        Sin' Mailie's dead.

Or, if he wanders up the howe,   glen
Her livin image in her yowe   ewe
Comes bleatin till him, owre the knowe,   knoll
        For bits o' bread;
An' down the briny pearls rowe   roll
        For Mailie dead.

She was nae get o' moorlan tips,   issue; tups [rams]
Wi' tawted ket, an' hairy hips;   matted fleece; rumps
For her forbears were brought in ships,
        Frae 'yont the Tweed:
A bonier fleesh ne'er cross'd the clips   fleece; shears
        Than Mailie's dead.

Woe befall Wae worth the man wha first did shape
dangerous That vile, wanchancie thing – a rape!
snarl in agony It maks guid fellows girn an' gape,
　　　　　　　　　Wi' chokin dread;
　An' Robin's bonnet wave wi' crape
　　　　　　　　　For Mailie dead.

　O a' ye bards on bonie Doon!
bagpipes An' wha on Ayr your chanters tune!
　Come, join the melancholious croon
　　　　　　　　　O' Robin's reed!
rejoice His heart will never get aboon!
　　　　　　　　　His Mailie's dead!

TO A MOUSE

ON TURNING HER UP IN HER NEST WITH THE PLOUGH, NOVEMBER 1785

Wee, sleekit, cowran, tim'rous beastie,   *sleek*
O, what a panic's in thy breastie!
Thou need na start awa sae hasty
         Wi' bickering brattle!   *hurrying scamper*
I wad be laith to rin an' chase thee,   *loth*
         Wi' murdering pattle!   *long-handled spade*

I'm truly sorry man's dominion
Has broken Nature's social union,
An' justifies that ill opinion
         Which makes thee startle
At me, thy poor, earth-born companion
         An' fellow mortal!

I doubt na, whyles, but thou may thieve;   *sometimes*
What then? poor beastie, thou maun live!   *must*
A daimen icker in a thrave   *odd ear; twenty-four*
         'S a sma' request;   *sheaves*
I'll get a blessin wi' the lave,   *remainder*
         An' never miss't!

Thy wee-bit housie, too, in ruin!
Its silly wa's the win's are strewin!   *feeble; winds*
An' naething, now, to big a new ane,   *build*
         O' foggage green!   *coarse grass*
An' bleak December's win's ensuin,
         Baith snell an' keen!   *bitter*

Thou saw the fields laid bare an' waste,
An' weary winter comin fast,
An' cozie here, beneath the blast,
         Thou thought to dwell,
Till crash! the cruel coulter past
         Out thro' thy cell.

stubble

That wee bit heap o' leaves an' stibble,
Has cost thee monie a weary nibble!
Now thou's turned out, for a' thy trouble,
          But house or hald,

Without; holding

To thole the winter's sleety dribble,

endure

             An' cranreuch cauld!

hoar-frost

But Mousie, thou art no thy lane,
In proving foresight may be vain:
The best-laid schemes o' mice an' men

alone

          Gang aft agley,
An' lea'e us nought but grief an' pain,

askew

            For promis'd joy!

Still, thou art blest, compared wi' me!
The present only toucheth thee:
But och! I backward cast my e'e,
          On prospects drear!
An' forward, tho' I canna see,
            I guess an' fear!

THE AULD FARMER'S
NEW-YEAR MORNING
SALUTATION TO HIS
AULD MARE, MAGGIE

ON GIVING HER THE
ACCUSTOMED RIPP OF CORN
TO HANSEL IN THE NEW-YEAR

A Guid New-Year I wish thee, Maggie!
Hae, there's a ripp to thy auld baggie: *handful of unthreshed*
Tho' thou's howe-backit now, an' knaggie,   *corn; belly*
           I've seen the day   *hollow-backed;*
           knobby
Thou could hae gaen like onie staggie,   *gone; colt*
           Out-owre the lay.   *beyond; lea*

Tho' now thou's dowie, stiff, an' crazy,   *dejected*
An' thy auld hide as white's a daisie,
I've seen thee dappl't, sleek an' glaizie,   *shiny*
           A bonie gray:
He should been tight that daur't to raize thee,   *prepared; excite*
           Ance in a day.

Thou ance was i' the foremost rank,
A filly buirdly, steeve, an' swank: *stalwart, firm and agile*
An' set weel down a shapely shank
           As e'er tread yird;   *earth*
An' could hae flown out-owre a stank   *pond*
           Like onie bird.

It's now some nine-an'-twenty year
Sin' thou was my guid-father's meere;   *father-in-law's*
He gied me thee, o' tocher clear,   *wholly as dowry*
           An' fifty mark;
Tho' it was sma', 'twas weel-won gear,
           An' thou was stark.   *strong*

When first I gaed to woo my Jenny,   *went*
Ye then was trottan wi' your minnie: *mother*
Tho' ye was trickie, slee, an' funnie,   *sly*
           Ye ne'er was donsie: *mischievous*
But hamely, tawie, quiet, an' cannie,   *tractable*
           An' unco sonsie.   *good-tempered*

67

That day, ye pranc'd wi' muckle pride,
When ye bure hame my bonie bride:
An' sweet an' gracefu' she did ride,
Wi' maiden air!
Kyle-Stewart I could braggèd wide,
For sic a pair.

bore — bore

have challenged

Tho' now ye dow but hoyte and hobble,
An' wintle like a saumont-coble,
That day, ye was a jinker noble,
For heels an' win'!
An' ran them till they a' did wauble,
Far, far behin'!

can; stumble
stagger; salmon-boat
goer
wind
wobble

When thou an' I were young and skiegh,
An' stable-meals at fairs were driegh,
How thou wad prance, an' snore, an' skriegh,
An' tak the road!
Town's-bodies ran, an' stood abiegh,
An' ca't thee mad.

skittish
tedious
snort; whinny

aloof

When thou was corn't, an' I was mellow,
We took the road ay like a swallow:
At brooses thou had ne'er a fellow,
For pith an' speed;
But ev'ry tail thou pay't them hollow,
Whare'er thou gaed.

wedding-races

The sma, droop-rumpl't, hunter cattle
Might aiblins waur't thee for a brattle;
But sax Scotch miles thou try't their mettle,
An' gar't them whaizle:
Nae whip nor spur, but just a wattle
O' saugh or hazle.

short-rumped
perhaps have beat;
spurt
wheeze

willow

Thou was a noble fittie-lan',
As e'er in tug or tow was drawn!
Aft thee an' I, in aught hours' gaun,
On guid March-weather,
Hae turn'd sax rood beside our han'
For days thegither.

near left-hand horse in
the plough
going

by ourselves

Thou never braing't, an' fetch't, an' fliskit,
But thy auld tail thou wad hae whiskit,
An' spread abreed thy weel-fill'd brisket,
Wi' pith an' pow'r;
Till sprittie knowes wad rair't, an' riskit,
An' slypet owre.

drew unsteadily;
stopped suddenly;
fretted

rushy hillocks would
have roared; cracked
fallen smoothly over

68

The Auld Farmer's Salutation

When frosts lay lang, an' snaws were deep,
An' threaten'd labour back to keep,
I gied thy cog a wee bit heap   dish
                   Aboon the timmer: edge
I ken'd my Maggie wad na sleep
                   For that, or simmer.   ere

In cart or car thou never reestit;
The steyest brae thou wad hae fac't it;   stiffest incline
Thou never lap, an' sten't, an' breastit,   leaped; sprang
                   Then stood to blaw;
But just thy step a wee thing hastit,
                   Thou snoov't awa.   jogged along

My pleugh is now thy bairntime a',   team; offspring
Four gallant brutes as e'er did draw;
Forby sax mae I've sell't awa,   more
                   That thou hast nurst:
They drew me thretteen pund an' twa,
                   The vera warst.

Monie a sair darg we twa hae wrought,   day's work
An' wi' the weary warl' fought!
An' monie an anxious day I thought
                   We wad be beat!
Yet here to crazy age we're brought,
                   Wi' something yet.

An' think na, my auld trusty servan',
That now perhaps thou's less deservin,
An' thy auld days may end in starvin;
                   For my last fow,   bushel
A heapet stimpart, I'll reserve ane   quarter-peck
                   Laid by for you.

We've worn to crazy years thegither;
We'll toyte about wi' ane anither;   totter
Wi' tentie care I'll flit thy tether   change
                   To some hain'd rig,   reserved patch
Whare ye may nobly rax your leather   fill your stomach
                   Wi' sma' fatigue.

Descriptive, Narrative and Celebratory Poems

THE COTTER'S SATURDAY NIGHT

INSCRIBED TO R. AIKEN, ESQ.

Let not Ambition mock their useful toil,
Their homely joys, and destiny obscure;
Nor Grandeur hear, with a disdainful smile,
The short and simple annals of the poor.

GRAY

1

My lov'd, my honor'd, much respected friend!
   No mercenary bard his homage pays;
With honest pride, I scorn each selfish end,
   My dearest meed, a friend's esteem and praise:
To you I sing, in simple Scottish lays,
   The lowly train in life's sequester'd scene;
The native feelings strong, the guileless ways;
   What Aiken in a cottage would have been;
Ah! tho' his worth unknown, far happier there I
   ween!

2

November chill blaws loud wi' angry sugh;   *wail*
   The short'ning winter-day is near a close;
The miry beasts retreating frae the pleugh;
   The black'ning trains o' craws to their repose:
The toil-worn Cotter frae his labor goes,
   This night his weekly moil is at an end,
Collects his spades, his mattocks, and his hoes,
   Hoping the morn in ease and rest to spend,
And weary, o'er the moor, his course does hameward
   bend.

3

At length his lonely cot appears in view,
  Beneath the shelter of an aged tree;
totter

Th' expectant wee-things, toddlin, stacher
    through
fluttering

To meet their dad, wi' flichterin' noise and glee.
His wee bit ingle, blinkin bonilie,
  His clean hearth-stane, his thrifty wifie's smile,
The lisping infant, prattling on his knee,
  Does a' his weary carking cares beguile,
And makes him quite forget his labor and his toil.

4

By and by
Belyve, the elder bairns come drapping in,
  At service out, amang the farmers roun';
follow; heedful run
Some ca' the pleugh, some herd, some tentie rin
quiet
  A cannie errand to a neebor toun:
Their eldest hope, their Jenny, woman grown,
  In youthfu' bloom, love sparkling in her e'e,
Comes hame, perhaps, to show a braw new gown,
hard-; wages
  Or deposite her sair-won penny-fee,
To help her parents dear, if they in hardship be.

5

With joy unfeign'd, brothers and sisters meet,
asks
  And each for other's weelfare kindly spiers:
The social hours, swift-wing'd, unnotic'd fleet;
strange news
  Each tells the uncos that he sees or hears.
The parents partial eye their hopeful years;
  Anticipation forward points the view;
The mother, wi' her needle and her sheers,
Makes; clothes
  Gars auld claes look amaist as weel's the new;
The father mixes a' wi' admonition due.

6

Their master's and their mistress's command
    The younkers a' are warned to obey;
And mind their labors wi' an eydent hand,   diligent
    And ne'er, tho' out o' sight, to jauk or play: trifle
"And O! be sure to fear the Lord alway,
    And mind your duty, duly, morn and night;
Lest in temptation's path ye gang astray,
    Implore His counsel and assisting might:
They never sought in vain that sought the Lord
    aright."

7

But hark! a rap comes gently to the door;
    Jenny, wha kens the meaning o' the same,
Tells how a neebor lad came o'er the moor,
    To do some errands, and convoy her hame.
The wily mother sees the conscious flame
    Sparkle in Jenny's e'e, and flush her cheek;
With heart-struck, anxious care, enquires his
    name,
    While Jenny hafflins is afraid to speak;   half
Weel-pleas'd the mother hears, it's nae wild, worth-
    less rake.

8

With kindly welcome, Jenny brings him ben;   inside
    A strappin' youth, he takes the mother's eye;
Blythe Jenny sees the visit's no ill taen;
    The father cracks of horses, pleughs, and kye.   chats; cattle
The youngster's artless heart o'erflows wi' joy,
    But blate and laithfu', scarce can weel behave; shy; sheepish
The mother, wi' a woman's wiles, can spy
    What makes the youth sae bashfu' and sae
    grave;
Weel-pleas'd to think her bairn's respected like the
    lave.   rest

9

O happy love! where love like this is found:
　　O heart-felt raptures! bliss beyond compare!
I've pacèd much this weary, mortal round,
　　And sage experience bids me this declare:
　　"If Heaven a draught of heavenly pleasure spare,
　　　One cordial in this melancholy vale,
　　'Tis when a youthful, loving, modest pair,
　　　In other's arms, breathe out the tender tale
Beneath the milk-white thorn that scents the ev'ning
　　gale."

10

Is there, in human form, that bears a heart,
　　A wretch! a villain! lost to love and truth!
That can, with studied, sly, ensnaring art,
　　Betray sweet Jenny's unsuspecting youth?
　　Curse on his perjur'd arts! dissembling, smooth!
　　　Are honor, virtue, conscience, all exil'd?
　　Is there no pity, no relenting ruth,
　　　Points to the parents fondling o'er their child?
Then paints the ruin'd maid, and their distraction
　　wild?

11

But now the supper crowns their simple board,
　　The healsome porritch, chief o' Scotia's food:
The soupe their only hawkie does afford,
　　That 'yont the hallan snugly chows her cood;
　　The dame brings forth, in complimental mood,
　　　To grace the lad, her weel-hain'd kebbuck, fell;
　　And aft he's prest, and aft he ca's it guid;
　　　The frugal wifie, garrulous, will tell,
How 'twas a towmond auld, sin' lint was i' the bell.

[gloss: wholesome]
[gloss: milk; cow]
[gloss: beyond; partition]
[gloss: -saved; cheese; pungent]
[gloss: twelve-month; flax; flower]

12

The chearfu' supper done, wi' serious face,
　　They, round the ingle, form a circle wide;
The sire turns o'er, wi' patriarchal grace,
　　The big ha'-Bible, ance his father's pride.
　　His bonnet rev'rently is laid aside,
　　　His lyart haffets wearing thin and bare;
　　Those strains that once did sweet in Zion glide,
　　　He wales a portion with judicious care,
"And let us worship God!" he says, with solemn air.

[gloss: grey side-locks]
[gloss: selects]

76

13

They chant their artless notes in simple guise;
  They tune their hearts, by far the noblest aim:
Perhaps *Dundee's* wild-warbling measures rise,
  Or plaintive *Martyrs*, worthy of the name;
Or noble *Elgin* beets the heaven-ward flame,   fans
  The sweetest far of Scotia's holy lays:
Compar'd with these, Italian trills are tame;
  The tickl'd ears no heart-felt raptures raise;
Nae unison hae they, with our Creator's praise.

14

The priest-like father reads the sacred page,
  How Abram was the friend of God on high;
Or, Moses bade eternal warfare wage
  With Amalek's ungracious progeny;
Or, how the royal Bard did groaning lie
  Beneath the stroke of Heaven's avenging ire;
Or Job's pathetic plaint, and wailing cry;
  Or rapt Isaiah's wild, seraphic fire;
Or other holy Seers that tune the sacred lyre.

15

Perhaps the Christian volume is the theme:
  How guiltless blood for guilty man was shed;
How He, who bore in Heaven the second name,
  Had not on earth whereon to lay His head;
How His first followers and servants sped;
  The precepts sage they wrote to many a land:
How he, who lone in Patmos banishèd,
  Saw in the sun a mighty angel stand,
And heard great Bab'lon's doom pronounc'd by
  Heaven's command.

16

Then kneeling down to Heaven's Eternal King,
    The saint, the father, and the husband prays:
Hope "springs exulting on triumphant wing,"*
    That thus they all shall meet in future days,
There, ever bask in uncreated rays,
    No more to sigh or shed the bitter tear,
Together hymning their Creator's praise,
    In such society, yet still more dear;
While circling Time moves round in an eternal
    sphere.

17

Compar'd with this, how poor Religion's pride,
    In all the pomp of method, and of art,
When men display to congregations wide
    Devotion's ev'ry grace, except the heart!
The Power, incens'd, the pageant will desert,
    The pompous strain, the sacerdotal stole;
But haply, in some cottage far apart,
    May hear, well-pleas'd, the language of the
    soul,
And in His Book of Life the inmates poor enroll.

18

Then homeward all take off their sev'ral way;
    The youngling cottagers retire to rest:
The parent-pair their secret homage pay,
    And proffer up to Heaven the warm request.
That He who stills the raven's clam'rous nest,
    And decks the lily fair in flow'ry pride,
Would, in the way His wisdom sees the best,
    For them and for their little ones provide;
But, chiefly, in their hearts with Grace divine
    preside.

* Pope's *Windsor Forest*. [Burns's note.]

19

From scenes like these, old Scotia's grandeur
    springs,
    That makes her lov'd at home, rever'd abroad:
Princes and lords are but the breath of kings,
    "An honest man's the noblest work of God";
And certes, in fair Virtue's heavenly road,
    The cottage leaves the palace far behind:
What is a lordling's pomp? a cumbrous load,
    Disguising oft the wretch of human kind,
Studied in arts of Hell, in wickedness refin'd!

20

O Scotia! my dear, my native soil!
    For whom my warmest wish to Heaven is sent!
Long may thy hardy sons of rustic toil
    Be blest with health and peace and sweet
        content!
And O! may Heaven their simple lives prevent
    From Luxury's contagion, weak and vile!
Then, how'er crowns and coronets be rent,
    A virtuous populace may rise the while,
And stand a wall of fire around their much-lov'd Isle.

21

O Thou! who pour'd the patriotic tide,
    That stream'd thro' great, unhappy Wallace'
        heart,
Who dar'd to, nobly, stem tyrannic pride,
    Or nobly die, the second glorious part:
(The patriot's God, peculiarly Thou art,
    His friend, inspirer, guardian, and reward!)
O never, never Scotia's realm desert;
    But still the patriot, and the patriot-bard
In bright succession raise, her ornament and guard!

TAM O' SHANTER

A Tale

Of Brownyis and of Bogillis full is this buke.
GAWIN DOUGLAS

pedlar fellows	When chapman billies leave the street,
thirsty	And drouthy neebors neebors meet;
	As market-days are wearing late,
road	An' folk begin to tak the gate;
ale	While we sit bousing at the nappy,
drunk; mighty	An' getting fou and unco happy,
not	We think na on the lang Scots miles,
bogs; pools; breaches;	The mosses, waters, slaps, and styles,
stiles	That lie between us and our hame,
	Whare sits our sulky, sullen dame,
	Gathering her brows like gathering storm,
	Nursing her wrath to keep it warm.
found	This truth fand honest Tam o' Shanter,
one	As he frae Ayr ae night did canter:
	(Auld Ayr, wham ne'er a town surpasses,
	For honest men and bonie lasses.)
	O Tam, had'st thou but been sae wise,
to have taken	As taen thy ain wife Kate's advice!
good-for-nothing	She tauld thee weel thou was a skellum,
chattering; babbler	A blethering, blustering, drunken blellum;
	That frae November till October,
	Ae market-day thou was nae sober;
every meal-grinding	That ilka melder wi' the miller,
money	Thou sat as lang as thou had siller;
called	That ev'ry naig was ca'd a shoe on,
	The smith and thee gat roaring fou on;
	That at the Lord's house, even on Sunday,
	Thou drank wi' Kirkton Jean till Monday.
	She prophesied, that, late or soon,
	Thou would be found deep drown'd in Doon,
dark	Or catch'd wi' warlocks in the mirk
	By Alloway's auld, haunted kirk.

Ah! gentle dames, it gars me greet,   makes; weep
To think how monie counsels sweet,
How monie lengthen'd, sage advices
The husband frae the wife despises!

But to our tale: Ae market-night,
Tam had got planted unco right,   uncommonly
Fast by an ingle, bleezing finely,
Wi' reaming swats, that drank divinely;   foaming new ale
And at his elbow, Souter Johnie,   Cobbler
His ancient, trusty, drouthy cronie: thirsty
Tam lo'ed him like a very brither;
They had been fou for weeks thegither.
The night drave on wi' sangs and clatter;
And ay the ale was growing better:
The landlady and Tam grew gracious
Wi' secret favours, sweet and precious:
The Souter tauld his queerest stories;
The landlord's laugh was ready chorus:
The storm without might rair and rustle,   roar
Tam did na mind the storm a whistle.

Care, mad to see a man sae happy,
E'en drown'd himsel amang the nappy.   ale
As bees flee hame wi' lades o' treasure,
The minutes wing'd their way wi' pleasure:
Kings may be blest but Tam was glorious,
O'er a' the ills o' life victorious!

But pleasures are like poppies spread:
You seize the flow'r, its bloom is shed;
Or like the snow falls in the river,
A moment white – then melts for ever;
Or like the Borealis race,
That flit ere you can point their place;
Or like the rainbow's lovely form
Evanishing amid the storm.
Nae man can tether time or tide;
The hour approaches Tam maun ride: must
That hour, o' night's black arch the key-stane,
That dreary hour Tam mounts his beast in;
And sic a night he taks the road in,
As ne'er poor sinner was abroad in.

would have

The wind blew as 'twad blawn its last;
The rattling showers rose on the blast;
The speedy gleams the darkness swallow'd;
Loud, deep, and lang the thunder bellow'd:
That night, a child might understand,
The Deil had business on his hand.

Weel mounted on his gray mare Meg,
A better never lifted leg,

spanked; puddle

Tam skelpit on thro' dub and mire,
Despising wind, and rain, and fire;

Now

Whiles holding fast his guid blue bonnet,

song

Whiles crooning o'er some auld Scots sonnet,

staring

Whiles glow'ring round wi' prudent cares,

ghosts

Lest bogles catch him unawares:
Kirk-Alloway was drawing nigh,

owls

Whare ghaists and houlets nightly cry.

across

By this time he was cross the ford,

smothered

Whare in the snaw the chapman smoor'd;

birches; big

And past the birks and meikle stane,
Whare drunken Charlie brak's neck-bane;

furze; pile of stones

And thro' the whins, and by the cairn,
Whare hunters fand the murder'd bairn;

above

And near the thorn, aboon the well,
Whare Mungo's mither hang'd hersel.
Before him Doon pours all his floods;
The doubling storm roars thro' the woods;
The lightnings flash from pole to pole;
Near and more near the thunders roll:
When, glimmering thro' the groaning trees,
Kirk-Alloway seemed in a bleeze,

chink

Thro' ilka bore the beams were glancing,
And loud resounded mirth and dancing.

Inspiring, bold John Barleycorn!
What dangers thou canst make us scorn!

ale

Wi' tippenny, we fear nae evil;

whisky

Wi' usquabae, we'll face the Devil!
The swats sae ream'd in Tammie's noddle,

not; farthing

Fair play, he car'd na deils a boddle.
But Maggie stood, right sair astonish'd,
Till, by the heel and hand admonish'd,
She ventur'd forward on the light;

wondrous

And, wow! Tam saw an unco sight!

82

Warlocks and witches in a dance:
Nae cotillion, brent new frae France,   brand
But hornpipes, jigs, strathspeys, and reels,
Put life and mettle in their heels.
A winnock-bunker in the east,   window-seat
There sat Auld Nick, in shape o' beast;
A tousie tyke, black, grim, and large,   shaggy dog
To gie them music was his charge:
He screw'd the pipes and gart them skirl,   shriek
Till roof and rafters a' did dirl.   ring
Coffins stood round, like open presses,   cupboards
That shaw'd the dead in their last dresses;
And, by some devilish cantraip sleight,   magic device
Each in its cauld hand held a light:
By which heroic Tam was able
To note upon the haly table,
A murderer's banes, in gibbet-airns;   -irons
Twa span-lang, wee, unchristen'd bairns;
A thief new-cutted frae a rape –
Wi' his last gasp his gab did gape;   mouth
Five tomahawks wi' bluid red-rusted;
Five scymitars wi' murder crusted;
A garter which a babe had strangled;
A knife a father's throat had mangled –
Whom his ain son o' life bereft –
The grey hairs yet stack to the heft;
Wi' mair of horrible and awefu',
Which even to name wad be unlawfu'.

As Tammie glowr'd, amaz'd, and curious,   stared
The mirth and fun grew fast and furious;
The piper loud and louder blew,
The dancers quick and quicker flew,
They reel'd, they set, they cross'd, they cleekit, took hold
Till ilka carlin swat and reekit,   each old woman
And coost her duddies to the wark,   sweated and steamed
And linket at it in her sark!   rags
                                             tripped; shift

Now Tam, O Tam, had thae been queans,   these; young girls
A' plump and strapping in their teens!
Their sarks, instead o' creeshie flannen,   greasy
Been snaw-white seventeen hunder linen!*

* Linen woven with 1,700 threads to the warp.

These

Thir breeks o' mine, my only pair,
That ance were plush, o' guid blue hair,

buttocks

I wad hae gi'en them off my hurdies

girls

For ae blink o' the bonie burdies!

But wither'd beldams, auld and droll,

Withered; wean

Rigwoodie hags wad spean a foal,

leaping; kicking;

Louping and flinging on a crummock,

cudgel

I wonder didna turn thy stomach!

well

But Tam kend what was what fu' brawlie:

comely; choice

There was ae winsome wench and wawlie,

company

That night enlisted in the core,
Lang after kend on Carrick shore

death

(For monie a beast to dead she shot,
An' perish'd monie a bonie boat,

much; barley

And shook baith meikle corn and bear,
And kept the country-side in fear.)

short shift; coarse
cloth

Her cutty sark, o' Paisley harn,
That while a lassie she had worn,
In longitude tho' sorely scanty,

proud

It was her best, and she was vauntie.
Ah! little kend thy reverend grannie,

bought

That sark she coft for her wee Nannie,
Wi' twa pund Scots ('twas a' her riches,)

Would have

Wad ever grac'd a dance of witches!

lower

But here my Muse her wing maun cour,
Sic flights as far beyond her power:

leaped and kicked

To sing how Nannie lap and flang
(A souple jad she was and strang;)
And how Tam stood like ane bewitch'd,

eyes

And thought his very een enrich'd;

twitched with excitement; jerked

Even Satan glowr'd, and fidg'd fu' fain,
And hotch'd and blew wi' might and main;

then

Till first ae caper, syne anither,

lost

Tam tint his reason a' thegither,
And roars out: "Weel done, Cutty-sark!"
And in an instant all was dark;
And scarcely had he Maggie rallied,
When out the hellish legion sallied.

As bees bizz out wi' angry fyke,   fret
When plundering herds assail their byke;   hive
As open pussie's mortal foes,   the hare's
When, pop! she starts before their nose;
As eager runs the market-crowd,
When "Catch the thief!" resounds aloud:
So Maggie runs, the witches follow,
Wi' mony an eldritch skreech and hollow.   unearthly

   Ah, Tam! Ah, Tam! thou'll get thy fairin!
In hell they'll roast thee like a herrin!
In vain thy Kate awaits thy comin!
Kate soon will be a woefu' woman!
Now, do thy speedy utmost, Meg,
And win the key-stane of the brig;
There, at them thou thy tail may toss,
A running stream they dare na cross!
But ere the key-stane she could make,
The fient a tail she had to shake: devil
For Nannie, far before the rest,
Hard upon noble Maggie prest,
And flew at Tam wi' furious ettle;   aim
But little wist she Maggie's mettle!
Ae spring brought off her master hale,   whole
But left behind her ain grey tail:
The carlin claught her by the rump,   seized
And left poor Maggie scarce a stump.

   Now, wha this tale o' truth shall read,
Ilk man, and mother's son, take heed:
Whene'er to drink you are inclin'd,
Or cutty sarks run in your mind,
Think! ye may buy the joys o'er dear:
Remember Tam o' Shanter's mare.

TO A HAGGIS

jolly

Fair fa' your honest, sonsie face,
Great chieftain o' the puddin-race!

Above
Paunch; small guts

Aboon them a' ye tak your place,
    Painch, tripe, or thairm:
Weel are ye wordy of a grace
    As lang's my arm.

buttocks
skewer

The groaning trencher there ye fill,
Your hurdies like a distant hill,
Your pin wad help to mend a mill
    In time o' need,
While thro' your pores the dews distil
    Like amber bead.

wipe
skill

His knife see rustic Labour dight,
An' cut ye up wi' ready slight,
Trenching your gushing entrails bright,
    Like onie ditch;
And then, O what a glorious sight,
    Warm-reekin, rich!

spoon

Then, horn for horn, they stretch an' strive:
Deil tak the hindmost, on they drive,

bellies; by and by

Till a' their weel-swall'd kytes belyve
    Are bent like drums;

burst

Then auld Guidman, maist like to rive,
    "Bethankit!" hums.

Is there that owre his French *ragout*,

sicken

Or *olio* that wad staw a sow,
Or *fricassee* wad mak her spew

disgust

    Wi' perfect sconner,
Looks down wi' sneering, scornfu' view
    On sic a dinner?

Poor devil! see him owre his trash,

weak; rush

As feckless as a wither'd rash,
His spindle shank a guid whip-lash,

fist; nut

    His nieve a nit;
Thro' bluidy flood or field to dash,
    O how unfit!

To a Haggis

But mark the Rustic, haggis-fed,
The trembling earth resounds his tread,
Clap in his walie nieve a blade,   ample
            He'll make it whissle;
An' legs, an' arms, an' heads will sned   crop
            Like taps o' thrissle.

Ye Pow'rs, wha mak mankind your care,
And dish them out their bill o' fare,
Auld Scotland wants nae skinking ware,   watery
            That jaups in luggies: splashes; bowl with
But, if ye wish her gratefu' prayer,   handles
            Gie her a Haggis!

Verse Letters

EPISTLE TO DAVIE, A BROTHER POET

1

While winds frae aff Ben-Lomond blaw,
And bar the doors wi' driving snaw,
  And hing us owre the ingle,   *fire*
I set me down to pass the time,
And spin a verse or twa o' rhyme,
  In hamely, westlin jingle: *westland*
While frosty winds blaw in the drift,   *Right to the chimney*
  Ben to the chimla lug,   *corner*
I grudge a wee the great-folk's gift,
  That live sae bien an' snug: *comfortable*
    I tent less, and want less   *value*
      Their roomy fire-side;
    But hanker, and canker,
      To see their cursed pride.

2

It's hardly in a body's pow'r,
To keep, at times, frae being sour,
  To see how things are shar'd;
How best o' chiels are whyles in want,   *chaps; sometimes*
While coofs on countless thousands rant,   *dolts; roister*
  And ken na how to wair't;   *spend*
But Davie lad, ne'er fash your head,   *trouble*
  Tho' we hae little gear;   *wealth*
We're fit to win our daily bread,
  As lang's we're hale and fier: *whole; sound*
    " Mair spier na, nor fear na",*   *ask not*
      Auld age ne'er mind a feg;   *fig*
    The last o't, the warst o't,
      Is only but to beg.

* A quotation from Allan Ramsay's poem "The Poet's Wish".

3

To lie in kilns and barns at e'en,
When banes are craz'd, and bluid is thin,
  Is, doubtless, great distress!
Yet then content could make us blest;
Ev'n then, sometimes, we'd snatch a taste
  Of truest happiness.
The honest heart that's free frae a'
  Intended fraud or guile,
However Fortune kick the ba',
  Has ay some cause to smile;
    And mind still, you'll find still,
     A comfort this nae sma';
    Nae mair then, we'll care then,
     Nae farther can we fa'.

4

What tho', like commoners of air,
We wander out, we know not where,
Without; holding   But either house or hal'?
Yet Nature's charms, the hills and woods,
The sweeping vales, and foaming floods,
  Are free alike to all.
In days when daisies deck the ground,
  And blackbirds whistle clear,
With honest joy our hearts will bound,
  To see the coming year:
hill-sides   On braes when we please then,
hum   We'll sit an' sowth a tune;
Then   Syne rhyme till't we'll time till't,
     An' sing't when we hae done.

5

It's no in titles nor in rank:
It's no in wealth like Lon'on Bank,
   To purchase peace and rest.
It's no in makin muckle, mair;   much, more
It's no in books, it's no in lear,   learning
   To make us truly blest:
If happiness hae not her seat
   An' centre in the breast,
We may be wise, or rich, or great,
   But never can be blest!
      Nae treasures nor pleasures
         Could make us happy lang;
      The heart ay's the part ay
         That makes us right or wrang.

6

Think ye, that sic as you and I,
Wha drudge and drive thro' wet and dry,
   Wi' never-ceasing toil;
Think ye, are we less blest than they,
Wha scarcely tent us in their way,   heed
   As hardly worth their while?
Alas! how oft, in haughty mood,
   God's creatures they oppress!
Or else, neglecting a' that's guid,
   They riot in excess!
      Baith careless and fearless
         Of either Heaven or Hell;
      Esteeming and deeming
         It a' an idle tale!

7

Then let us cheerfu' acquiesce,
Nor make our scanty pleasures less
    By pining at our state:
And, even should misfortunes come,
I here wha sit hae met wi' some,

And am
        An's thankfu' for them yet.
They gie the wit of age to youth;
    They let us ken oursel;
They make us see the naked truth,
    The real guid and ill:
        Tho' losses and crosses
            Be lessons right severe,
        There's wit there, ye'll get there,
            Ye'll find nae other where.

8

listen to
cards
But tent me, Davie, ace o' hearts!
(To say aught less wad wrang the cartes,
    And flatt'ry I detest)
This life has joys for you and I;
And joys that riches ne'er could buy,
    And joys the very best.
There's a' the pleasures o' the heart,
    The lover an' the frien':
Ye hae your Meg, your dearest part,
    And I my darling Jean!
        It warms me, it charms me
            To mention but her name:
kindles
        It heats me, it beets me,
            And sets me a' on flame!

9

O all ye Pow'rs who rule above!
O Thou whose very self art love!
   Thou know'st my words sincere!
The life-blood streaming thro' my heart,
Or my more dear immortal part,
   Is not more fondly dear!
When heart-corroding care and grief
   Deprive my soul of rest,
Her dear idea brings relief
   And solace to my breast.
     Thou Being All-seeing,
       O, hear my fervent pray'r!
     Still take her, and make her
       Thy most peculiar care!

10

All hail! ye tender feelings dear!
The smile of love, the friendly tear,
   The sympathetic glow!
Long since, this world's thorny ways
Had number'd out my weary days,
   Had it not been for you!
Fate still has blest me with a friend
   In every care and ill;
And oft, a more endearing band,
   A tie more tender still.
     It lightens, it brightens
       The tenebrific scene,
     To meet with, and greet with
       My Davie or my Jean!

O, how that Name inspires my style!

spanking · The words come skelpin' rank an' file,
    Amaist before I ken!
The ready measure rins as fine,
As Phoebus and the famous Nine

overlooking ·   Were glowrin owre my pen.
spavined · My spavet Pegasus will limp,
hot ·   Till ance he's fairly het;
hobble; limp; jump · And then he'll hilch, an' stilt, an' jimp,
uncommon burst ·   And rin an unco fit;
      But least then, the beast then
        Should rue this hasty ride,
wipe ·   I'll light now, and dight now
        His sweaty, wizen'd hide.

EPISTLE TO J. LAPRAIK

AN OLD SCOTTISH BARD,
APRIL 1, 1785

While briers an' woodbines budding green,
And paitricks scraichan loud at e'en,   *partridges calling*
An' morning poussie whiddan seen,   *the hare scudding*
         Inspire my Muse,
This freedom, in an unknown frien'
         I pray excuse.

On Fasten-e'en we had a rockin,   *Shrove Tuesday;*
To ca' the crack and weave our stockin;   *meeting*
And there was muckle fun and jokin,   *have a chat*
         Ye need na doubt;
At length we had a hearty yokin,   *set-to*
         At "sang about."

There was ae sang, amang the rest,   *one*
Aboon them a' it pleas'd me best,   *Above*
That some kind husband had addrest
         To some sweet wife:
It thirl'd the heart-strings thro' the breast,   *thrilled*
         A' to the life.

I've scarce heard ought describ'd sae weel,
What gen'rous, manly bosoms feel;
Thought I, "Can this be Pope or Steele,
         Or Beattie's wark?"
They tald me 'twas an odd kind chiel   *chap*
         About Muirkirk.

     twitching with excitement
It pat me fidgin-fain to hear't,
An' sae about him there I spier't;   *asked*
Then a' that kent him round declar'd
         He had ingine;
That nane excell'd it, few cam near't,   *talent*
         It was sae fine:

sober

That set him to a pint of ale,
An' either douce or merry tale,
Or rhymes an' sangs he'd made himsel,
   Or witty catches,
'Tween Inverness an' Teviotdale,
   He had few matches.

swore
harness
hawker
Behind a low wall

Then up I gat, an' swoor an aith,
Tho' I should pawn my pleugh an' graith,
Or die a cadger pownie's death,
   At some dyke-back,
A pint an' gill I'd gie them baith,

talk

   To hear your crack.

But, first an' foremost, I should tell,
Amaist as soon as I could spell,

rhyming

I to the crambo-jingle fell;
   Tho' rude an' rough,

humming

Yet crooning to a body's sel,
   Does weel eneugh.

I am nae poet, in a sense,
But just a rhymer like by chance,
An' hae to learning nae pretence,
   Yet, what the matter?
Whene'er my Muse does on me glance,
   I jingle at her.

Your critic-folk may cock their nose,
And say, "How can you e'er propose,
You wha ken hardly verse frae prose,
   To mak a sang?"
But, by your leaves, my learned foes,
   Ye're maybe wrang.

What's a' your jargon o' your Schools,
Your Latin names for horns an' stools?
If honest Nature made you fools,

serves

   What sairs your grammers?
Ye'd better taen up spades and shools,

stone-breaking

   Or knappin-hammers.

Epistle to J. Lapraik

A set o' dull, conceited hashes   *dunderheads*
Confuse their brains in college-classes.
They gang in stirks, and come out asses,   *young bullocks*
        Plain truth to speak;
An' syne they think to climb Parnassus   *then*
        By dint o' Greek!

Gie me ae spark o' Nature's fire,
That's a' the learning I desire;
Then, tho' I drudge thro' dub an' mire   *puddle*
        At pleugh or cart,
My Muse, tho' hamely in attire,
        May touch the heart.

O for a spunk o' Allan's glee,   *spark*
Or Fergusson's, the bauld an' slee,   *sly*
Or bright Lapraik's, my friend to be,
        If I can hit it!
That would be lear enough for me,   *learning*
        If I could get it.

Now, sir, if ye hae friends enow,
Tho' real friends I b'lieve are few,
Yet, if your catalogue be fow,   *full*
        I'se no insist: *I'll*
But, gif ye want ae friend that's true,
        I'm on your list.

I winna blaw about mysel,   *brag*
As ill I like my fauts to tell;
But friends, an' folks that wish me well,
        They sometimes roose me;   *praise*
Tho', I maun own, as monie still
        As far abuse me.

There's ae wee faut they whyles lay to me,
I like the lasses – Gude forgie me!   *God*
For monie a plack they wheedle frae me *coin*
        At dance or fair:
Maybe some ither thing they gie me,
        They weel can spare.

99

But Mauchline Race or Mauchline Fair,
I should be proud to meet you there;
We'se gie ae night's discharge to care,
        If we forgather;
And hae a swap o' rhymin-ware
        Wi' ane anither.

We'll

The four-gill chap, we'se gar him clatter,
An' kirsen him wi' reekin water;
Syne we'll sit down an' tak our whitter,
        To cheer our heart;
An' faith, we'se be acquainted better
        Before we part.

four-gill cup, we'll make
christen; steaming draught

Awa ye selfish, warly race,
Wha think that havins, sense, an' grace,
Ev'n love an' friendship should give place
        To Catch-the-Plack!
I dinna like to see your face,
        Nor hear your crack.

worldly
manners

the hunt for coin

But ye whom social pleasure charms,
Whose hearts the tide of kindness warms,
Who hold your being on the terms,
        "Each aid the others,"
Come to my bowl, come to my arms,
        My friends, my brothers!

But, to conclude my lang epistle,
As my auld pen's worn to the grissle,
Twa lines frae you wad gar me fissle,
        Who am most fervent,
While I can either sing or whistle,
        Your friend and servant.

tingle

SECOND EPISTLE TO
J. LAPRAIK

APRIL 21, 1785

While new-ca'd kye rowte at the stake	new-driven; low
An' pownies reek in pleugh or braik,	smoke; harrow
This hour on e'enin's edge I take,	
To own I'm debtor	
To honest-hearted, auld Lapraik,	
For his kind letter.	

Forjesket sair, with weary legs,	Jaded
Rattlin the corn out-owre the rigs,	ridges
Or dealing thro' amang the naigs	distributing
Their ten-hours' bite,	
My awkart Muse sair pleads and begs,	
I would na write.	

The tapetless, ramfeezl'd hizzie,	feckless, exhausted girl
She's saft at best an' something lazy;	
Quo' she: "Ye ken we've been sae busy	
This month an' mair,	
That trowth, my head is grown right dizzie,	
An' something sair."	

Her dowff excuses pat me mad:	dull
"Conscience," says I, "ye thowless jad!	lazy
I'll write, an' that a hearty blaud,	screed
This vera night;	
So dinna ye affront your trade,	do not
But rhyme it right.	

"Shall bauld Lapraik, the king o' hearts,	
Tho' mankind were a pack o' cartes,	
Roose you sae weel for your deserts,	Praise
In terms sae friendly;	
Yet ye'll neglect to shaw your parts	
An' thank him kindly?"	

twinkling	Sae I gat paper in a blink
	An' down gaed stumpie in the ink:
	Quoth I: "Before I sleep a wink,
	I vow I'll close it:
rhyme	An' if ye winna make it clink,
	By Jove, I'll prose it!"

Sae I've begun to scrawl, but whether
In rhyme, or prose, or baith thegither,
Or some hotch-potch that's rightly neither,
        Let time mak proof;
nonsense   But I shall scribble down some blether
off-hand   Just clean aff-loof.

My worthy friend, ne'er grudge an' carp,
Tho' Fortune use you hard an' sharp;
tickle   Come, kittle up your moorland harp
        Wi' gleesome touch!
woof   Ne'er mind how Fortune waft an' warp;
        She's but a bitch.

jerk; scare   She's gien me monie a jirt an' fleg,
straddle   Sin' I could striddle owre a rig;
    But, by the Lord, tho' I should beg
grey head   Wi' lyart pow,
dance   I'll laugh an' sing, an' shake my leg,
can   As lang's I dow!

Now comes the sax-an-twentieth simmer
trees   I've seen the bud upo' the timmer,
jade   Still persecuted by the limmer
        Frae year to year;
fickle gossip   But yet, despite the kittle kimmer,
        I, Rob, am here.

Do ye envý the city gent,
counter; cheat   Behint a kist to lie an' sklent;
Or purse-proud, big wi' cent per cent.
stomach   An' muckle wame,
burgh   In some bit brugh to represent
magistrate's   A bailie's name?

haughty   Or is't the paughty feudal thane,
shirt; shining   Wi' ruffl'd sark an' glancing cane,
Wha thinks himsel nae sheep-shank bane,
        But lordly stalks,
While caps an' bonnets off are taen,
        As by he walks?

Second Epistle to J. Lapraik

"O Thou wha gies us each guid gift!
Gie me o' wit an' sense a lift,   load
Then turn me, if Thou please, adrift
      Thro' Scotland wide;
Wi' cits nor lairds I wadna shift,
      In a' their pride!"

Were this the charter of our state,
"On pain o' hell be rich an' great,"
Damnation then would be our fate,
      Beyond remead;   remedy
But, thanks to heaven, that's no the gate   way
      We learn our creed.

For thus the royal mandate ran,
When first the human race began:
"The social, friendly, honest man,
      Whate'er he be,
'Tis he fulfils great Nature's plan,
      And none but he."

O mandate glorious and divine!
The followers o' the ragged Nine,
Poor, thoughtless devils! yet may shine
      In glorious light;
While sordid sons o' Mammon's line
      Are dark as night!

Tho' here they scrape, an' squeeze, an' growl,
Their worthless nievefu' of a soul   fistful
May in some future carcase howl,
      The forest's fright;
Or in some day-detesting owl
      May shun the light.

Then may Lapraik and Burns arise,
To reach their native, kindred skies,
And sing their pleasures, hopes an' joys,
      In some mild sphere;
Still closer knit in friendship's ties,
      Each passing year!

103

TO WILLIAM SIMPSON
OF OCHILTREE

MAY, 1785

I gat your letter, winsome Willie;
handsomely   Wi' gratefu' heart I thank you brawlie;
Tho' I maun say't, I wad be silly
mighty   And unco vain,
fellow   Should I believe, my coaxin billie,
                Your flatterin strain.

But I'se believe ye kindly meant it:
I'll   I sud be laith to think ye hinted
sideways squinted   Ironic satire, sidelins sklented,
                On my poor Musie;
extravagant   Tho' in sic phraisin terms ye've penn'd it,
                I scarce excuse ye.

wicker basket   My senses wad be in a creel,*
climb   Should I but dare a hope to speel,
Wi' Allan, or wi' Gilbertfield,
                The braes o' fame;
lawyer-chap   Or Fergusson, the writer-chiel,
                A deathless name.

(O Fergusson! thy glorious parts
Ill suited law's dry, musty arts!
whinstone   My curse upon your whunstane hearts
                Ye E'nbrugh gentry!
The tythe o' what ye waste at cartes
Would have stored   Wad stow'd his pantry!)

Yet when a tale comes i' my head,
rent   Or lasses gie my heart a screed,
sometimes; death   As whyles they're like to be my dead,
                (O sad disease!)
tickle   I kittle up my rustic reed;
                It gies me ease.

* The meaning of the whole line is "I'd be crazy".

To William Simpson

Auld Coila, now, may fidge fu' fain,   *twitch with delight*
She's gotten bardies o' her ain;
Chiels wha their chanters winna hain,   *spare*
              But tune their lays,
Till echoes a' resound again
              Her weel-sung praise.

Nae Poet thought her worth his while,
To set her name in measur'd style;
She lay like some unkend-of isle
              Beside New Holland,
Or whare wild-meeting oceans boil
              Besouth Magellan.   *South of*

Ramsay an' famous Fergusson
Gied Forth an' Tay a lift aboon;   *a lift-up*
Yarrow an' Tweed, to monie a tune,
              Owre Scotland rings;
While Irwin, Lugar, Ayr, an' Doon
              Naebody sings.

Th' Illissus, Tiber, Thames, an' Seine,
Glide sweet in monie a tunefu' line:
But, Willie, set your fit to mine,   *foot*
              An' cock your crest!
We'll gar our streams and burnies shine   *make; brooklets*
              Up wi' the best.

We'll sing auld Coila's plains an' fells,
Her moors red-brown wi' heather bells,
Her banks an' braes, her dens an' dells,   *hill-sides*
              Whare glorious Wallace
Aft bure the gree, as story tells,   *bore off the prize*
              Frae Suthron billies.

At Wallace' name, what Scottish blood
But boils up in a spring-tide flood?
Oft have our fearless fathers strode
              By Wallace' side,
Still pressing onward, red-wat-shod,   *shod with red blood*
              Or glorious dy'd!

river-meadows	O, sweet are Coila's haughs an' woods,
linnets	When lintwhites chant amang the buds,
sporting; gambols	And jinkin hares, in amorous whids,
	Their loves enjoy;
wood-pigeon coos	While thro' the braes the cushat croods
	With wailfu' cry!

Ev'n winter bleak has charms to me,
When winds rave thro' the naked tree;
Or frosts on hills of Ochiltree
    Are hoary gray;
Or blinding drifts wild-furious flee,
    Dark'ning the day!

O Nature! a' thy shews an' forms
To feeling, pensive hearts hae charms!
Whether the summer kindly warms,
    Wi' life an' light;
Or winter howls, in gusty storms,
    The lang, dark night!

found	The Muse, nae poet ever fand her,
	Till by himsel he learn'd to wander,
brook's	Adown some trottin burn's meander,
	An' no think lang:
	O sweet, to stray an' pensive ponder
	A heart-felt sang!

worldly	The warly race may drudge an' drive,
push; ply the elbows	Hog-shouther, jundie, stretch, an' strive;
describe	Let me fair Nature's face descrive,
	And I, wi' pleasure,
	Shall let the busy, grumbling hive
Hum	Bum owre their treasure.

	Fareweel, my rhyme-composing brither!
too long	We've been owre lang unkend to ither:
	Now let us lay our heads thegither,
	In love fraternal:
dangle in a rope	May Envy wallop in a tether,
	Black fiend, infernal!

To William Simpson

While Highlandmen hate tolls an' taxes;
While moorlan' herds like guid, fat braxies;   dead sheep
While Terra Firma, on her axis,
                    Diurnal turns;
Count on a friend, in faith an' practice,
                    In Robert Burns.

TO JAMES SMITH

Friendship, mysterious cement of the soul!
Sweet'ner of Life, and solder of Society!
I owe thee much——

BLAIR

cunning	Dear Smith, the slee'st, pawkie thief,
plunder	That e'er attempted stealth or rief!
wizard-spell	Ye surely hae some warlock-breef
	Owre human hearts;
proof	For ne'er a bosom yet was prief
	Against your arts.

For me, I swear by sun an' moon,
above   And ev'ry star that blinks aboon,
Ye've cost me twenty pair o' shoon,
going   Just gaun to see you;
And ev'ry ither pair that's done,
taken   Mair taen I'm wi' you.

gossip   That auld, capricious carlin, Nature,
stunted   To mak amends for scrimpit stature,
She's turn'd you off, a human-creature
      On her first plan;
And in her freaks, on ev'ry feature
      She's wrote the Man.

Just now I've taen the fit o' rhyme,
seething brain   My barmie noddle's working prime,
My fancy yerkit up sublime,
      Wi' hasty summon:
Hae ye a leisure-moment's time
      To hear what's comin?

Some rhyme a neebor's name to lash;
Some rhyme (vain thought!) for needfu' cash:
talk   Some rhyme to court the countra clash,
      An' raise a din;
trouble about   For me, an aim I never fash;
      I rhyme for fun.

To James Smith

The star that rules my luckless lot,
Has fated me the russet coat,
An' damn'd my fortune to the groat;
      But, in requit,
Has blest me with a random-shot
      O' countra wit.

This while my notion's taen a sklent,   *turn*
To try my fate in guid, black prent;
But still the mair I'm that way bent,
      Something cries, "Hoolie!   *Softly!*
I red you, honest man, tak tent!   *heed*
      Ye'll shaw your folly:

"There's ither poets, much your betters,
Far seen in Greek, deep men o' letters,
Hae thought they had ensur'd their debtors,
      A' future ages;
Now moths deform, in shapeless tatters,
      Their unknown pages."

Then farewell hopes o' laurel-boughs
To garland my poetic brows!
Henceforth I'll rove where busy ploughs
      Are whistling thrang;   *busily*
An' teach the lanely heights an' howes   *hollows*
      My rustic sang.

I'll wander on, wi' tentless heed   *careless*
How never-halting moments speed,
Till Fate shall snap the brittle thread;
      Then, all unknown,
I'll lay me with th' inglorious dead,
      Forgot and gone!

But why o' death begin a tale?
Just now we're living sound an' hale;   *well*
Then top and maintop crowd the sail,
      Heave Care o'er-side!
And large, before Enjoyment's gale,
      Let's tak the tide.

This life, sae far's I understand,
Is a' enchanted fairy-land,
Where Pleasure is the magic-wand,
    That, wielded right,
Maks hours like minutes, hand in hand,
    Dance by fu' light.

climbed   The magic-wand then let us wield;
     For, ance that five-an'-forty's speel'd,
Old Age   See, crazy, weary, joyless Eild,
       Wi' wrinkl'd face,
coughing, limping Comes hostin, hirplin owre the field,
      Wi' creepin pace.

twilight   When ance life's day draws near the gloamin,
     Then fareweel vacant, careless roamin;
An' fareweel cheerfu' tankards foamin,
    An' social noise:
An' fareweel dear, deluding Woman,
    The joy of joys!

O Life! how pleasant, in thy morning,
Young Fancy's rays the hills adorning!
Cold-pausing Caution's lesson scorning,
    We frisk away,
Like school-boys, at th' expected warning,
    To joy an' play.

We wander there, we wander here,
We eye the rose upon the brier,
Unmindful that the thorn is near,
    Among the leaves:
And tho' the puny wound appear,
    Short while it grieves.

    Some, lucky, find a flow'ry spot,
sweated   For which they never toil'd nor swat;
    They drink the sweet and eat the fat,
Without   But care or pain;
    And haply eye the barren hut
      With high disdain.

To James Smith

With steady aim, some Fortune chase;
Keen Hope does ev'ry sinew brace;
Thro' fair, thro' foul, they urge the race,
      And seize the prey:
Then cannie, in some cozie place,   *quiet; snug*
      They close the day.

And others like your humble servan',
Poor wights! nae rules nor roads observin,
To right or left eternal swervin,
      They zig-zag on;
Till, curst with age, obscure an' starvin,
      They aften groan.

Alas! what bitter toil an' straining –
But truce with peevish, poor complaining!
Is Fortune's fickle *Luna* waning?
      E'en let her gang!
Beneath what light she has remaining,
      Let's sing our sang.

My pen I here fling to the door,
And kneel, ye Pow'rs! and warm implore,
"Tho' I should wander *Terra* o'er,
      In all her climes,
Grant me but this, I ask no more,
      Ay rowth o' rhymes.   *plenty*

"Gie dreepin roasts to countra lairds,   *dripping*
Till icicles hing frae their beards;
Gie fine braw claes to fine life-guards   *clothes*
      And maids of honor;
And yill an' whisky gie to cairds,   *ale; tinkers*
      Until they sconner.   *sicken*

"A title, Dempster* merits it;
A garter gie to Willie Pitt;
Gie wealth to some be-ledger'd cit,
      In cent per cent;
But give me real, sterling wit,
      And I'm content.

* George Dempster, M.P. for Forfar Burghs, a noted agricultural improver.

"While ye are pleas'd to keep me hale,
I'll sit down o'er my scanty meal,

meal and water; beef-
less broth

Be't water-brose or muslin-kail,
           Wi' cheerfu' face,
As lang's the Muses dinna fail
           To say the grace."

An anxious e'e I never throws

ear

Behint my lug, or by my nose;

duck

I jouk beneath Misfortune's blows
           As weel's I may;
Sworn foe to sorrow, care, and prose,
           I rhyme away.

sedate

O ye douce folk that live by rule,
Grave, tideless-blooded, calm an' cool,
Compar'd wi' you – O fool! fool! fool!
           How much unlike!

wall

Your hearts are just a standing pool,
           Your lives a dyke!

Nae hair-brained, sentimental traces
In your unletter'd, nameless faces!
In *arioso* trills and graces
           Ye never stray;
But *gravissimo*, solemn basses
           Ye hum away.

Ye are sae grave, nae doubt ye're wise;

marvel

Nae ferly tho' ye do despise

headstrong

The hairum-scairum, ram-stam boys,
           The rattling squad:
I see ye upward cast your eyes –
           Ye ken the road!

hold

Whilst I – but I shall haud me there,
Wi' you I'll scarce gang ony where –
Then, Jamie, I shall say nae mair,

quit

           But quat my sang.
Content wi' you to mak a pair,
           Whare'er I gang.

Songs

LOVE AND LIBERTY

A Cantata

RECITATIVO

When lyart leaves bestrow the yird,	withered; ground
Or, wavering like the bauckie-bird,	bat
Bedim cauld Boreas' blast;	
When hailstanes drive wi' bitter skyte,	lash
And infant frosts begin to bite,	
In hoary cranreuch drest;	hoar-frost
Ae night at e'en a merry core	One; gang
O' randie, gangrel bodies	riotous, vagrant
In Poosie-Nansie's held the splore,	carousal
To drink their orra duddies:	spare rags
Wi' quaffing and laughing	
They ranted an' they sang,	roistered
Wi' jumping an' thumping	
The vera girdle rang.	very

First, niest the fire, in auld red rags	next
Ane sat, weel brac'd wi' mealy bags	
And knapsack a' in order;	
His doxy lay within his arm;	
Wi' usquebae an' blankets warm,	whisky
She blinket on her sodger.	leered
An' ay he gies the tozie drab	flushed with drink
The tither skelpan kiss,	sounding
While she held up her greedy gab	mouth
Just like an aumous dish:	alms-dish
Ilk smack still did crack still	Each
Like onie cadger's whup;	hawker's
Then, swaggering an' staggering,	
He roar'd this ditty up:	

115

SONG

TUNE: *Soldier's Joy*

I am a son of Mars, who have been in many wars,
    And show my cuts and scars wherever I come:
This here was for a wench, and that other in a trench
    When welcoming the French at the sound of the
        drum.

        Lal de daudle, &c.

My prenticeship I past, where my leader breath'd
    his last,
    When the bloody die was cast on the heights of
    Abram;*
And I servèd out my trade when the gallant game
    was play'd,
And the Moro† low was laid at the sound of the
    drum.

I lastly was with Curtis‡ among the floating batt'ries,
    And there I left for witness an arm and a limb;
Yet let my country need me, with Eliott to head me
    I'd clatter on my stumps at the sound of the drum.

And now, tho' I must beg with a wooden arm and
    leg
    And many a tatter'd rag hanging over my bum,
I'm as happy with my wallet, my bottle, and my
trull   callet
    As when I us'd in scarlet to follow a drum.

What tho' with hoary locks I must stand the winter
    shocks,
    Beneath the woods and rocks oftentimes for a
    home?
When the tother bag I sell, and the tother bottle tell,
    I could meet a troop of Hell at the sound of a drum.

* General Wolfe scaled the Heights of Abraham and took Quebec in September 1759.
† Fortress defending the harbour of Santiago, Cuba, stormed by the British in 1762.
‡ Admiral Sir Roger Curtis who broke the siege of Gibraltar by the French and Spanish in 1782.

Love and Liberty

RECITATIVO

He ended; and the kebars sheuk   rafters shook
    Aboon the chorus roar;   Over
While frighted rattons backward leuk,   rats
    An' seek the benmost bore: inmost hole
A fairy fiddler frae the neuk,   tiny; corner
    He skirl'd out *Encore!*   yelled
But up arose the martial chuck,   dear
    An' laid the loud uproar:

SONG

TUNE: *Sodger Laddie*

I once was a maid, tho' I cannot tell when,
And still my delight is in proper young men.
Some one of a troop of dragoons was my daddie:
No wonder I'm fond of a sodger laddie.
                Sing, lal de lal, &c.

The first of my loves was a swaggering blade,
To rattle the thundering drum was his trade;
His leg was so tight, and his cheek was so ruddy,
Transported I was with my sodger laddie.

But the godly old chaplain left him in the lurch:
The sword I forsook for the sake of the church;
He riskèd the soul, and I ventur'd the body:
'Twas then I prov'd false to my sodger laddie.

Full soon I grew sick of my sanctified sot,
The regiment at large for a husband I got;
From the gilded spontoon to the fife I was ready:
I askèd no more but a sodger laddie.

But the Peace it reduc'd me to beg in despair,
Till I met my old boy in a Cunningham* Fair;
His rags regimental they flutter'd so gaudy:
My heart it rejoic'd at a sodger laddie.

And now I have liv'd – I know not how long!
But still I can join in a cup and a song;
And whilst with both hands I can hold the glass
    steady,
Here's to thee, my hero, my sodger laddie!

* The northern district of Ayrshire.

117

RECITATIVO

Poor Merry-Andrew in the neuk
    Sat guzzling wi' a tinkler-hizzie;
tinker-wench
cared not; took

They mind't na wha the chorus teuk,
    Between themselves they were sae busy.
    At length, wi' drink an' courting dizzy,
struggled   He stoiter'd up an' made a face;
    Then turn'd an' laid a smack on Grizzie,
Then   Syne tun'd his pipes wi' grave grimace:

SONG

TUNE: *Auld Sir Symon*

drunk   Sir Wisdom's a fool when he's fou;
court   Sir Knave is a fool in a session:
He's there but a prentice I trow,
    But I am a fool by profession.

book   My grannie she bought me a beuk,
went off   An' I held awa to the school:
I fear I my talent misteuk,
    But what will ye hae of a fool?

For drink I wad venture my neck;
    A hizzie's the half of my craft:
But what could ye other expect
    Of ane that's avowedly daft?

bullock   I ance was tyed up like a stirk
    For civilly swearing and quaffing;
rebuked   I ance was abus'd i' the kirk
rumpling; fun For towsing a lass i' my daffin.

Poor Andrew that tumbles for sport
    Let naebody name wi' a jeer:
There's even, I'm tauld, i' the Court
    A tumbler ca'd the Premier.

Observ'd ye yon reverend lad
    Mak faces to tickle the mob?
He rails at our mountebank squad –
    It's rivalship just i' the job!

And now my conclusion I'll tell,
    For faith! I'm confoundedly dry:
fellow   The chiel that's a fool for himself,
    Guid Lord! he's far dafter than I.

Love and Liberty

RECITATIVO

Then niest outspak a raucle carlin,	sturdy old woman
Wha kent fu' weel to cleek the sterlin,	
For monie a pursie she had hookèd,	
An' had in monie a well been doukèd.	ducked
Her love had been a Highland laddie,	
But weary fa' the waefu' woodie!	plague upon; gallows
Wi' sighs an' sobs she thus began	
To wail her braw John Highlandman:	fine

SONG

TUNE: *O, An' Ye Were Dead, Guidman*

CHORUS

Sing hey my braw John Highlandman!
Sing ho my braw John Highlandman!
There's not a lad in a' the lan'
Was match for my John Highlandman.

A Highland lad my love was born,	
The lalland laws he held in scorn,	lowland
But he still was faithfu' to his clan,	
My gallant, braw John Highlandman.	

Sing hey &c.

With his philibeg, an' tartan plaid,	kilt
An' guid claymore down by his side,	
The ladies' hearts he did trepan,	
My gallant, braw John Highlandman.	

Sing hey &c.

We rangèd a' from Tweed to Spey,
An' liv'd like lords an' ladies gay,
For a lalland face he fearèd none,
My gallant, braw John Highlandman.

Sing hey &c.

They banish'd him beyond the sea,
But ere the bud was on the tree,
Adown my cheeks the pearls ran,
Embracing my John Highlandman.

Sing hey &c.

But Och! they catch'd him at the last,
And bound him in a dungeon fast.
My curse upon them every one –
They've hang'd my braw John Highlandman!

Sing hey &c.

And now a widow I must mourn
The pleasures that will ne'er return;
No comfort but a hearty can
When I think on John Highlandman.
Sing hey &c.

RECITATIVO

saunter
buxom

A pigmy scraper wi' his fiddle,
Wha us'd to trystes an' fairs to driddle,
Her strappin limb an' gawsie middle
(He reach'd nae higher)
Had hol'd his heartie like a riddle,

blown it
An' blawn't on fire.

hip
hummed

Wi' hand on hainch and upward e'e,
He croon'd his gamut, one, two, three,
Then in an *arioso* key
The wee Apollo
Set off wi' *allegretto* glee
His *giga* solo:

SONG

rest
TUNE: *Whistle Owre the Lave O't*

CHORUS

I am a fiddler to my trade,
An' a' the tunes that e'er I play'd,
The sweetest still to wife or maid
Was Whistle Owre the Lave O't.

reach; wipe

Let me ryke up to dight that tear;
An' go wi' me an' be my dear,
An' then your every care an' fear
May whistle owre the lave o't.
I am &c.

harvest-homes;
we'll

At kirns an' weddins we'se be there,
An' O, sae nicely 's we will fare!
We'll bowse about till Daddie Care
Sing *Whistle Owre the Lave O't.*
I am &c.

bones; pick
fence

Sae merrily the banes we'll pyke,
An' sun oursels about the dyke;
An' at our leisure, when ye like,
We'll – whistle owre the lave o't!
I am &c.

120

Love and Liberty

But bless me wi' your heav'n o' charms,
An' while I kittle hair on thairms,   tickle; catgut
Hunger, cauld, an' a' sic harms   such
    May whistle owre the lave o't.
                   I am &c.

RECITATIVO

Her charms had struck a sturdy caird   tinker
    As weel as poor gut-scraper;
He taks the fiddler by the beard,
    An' draws a roosty rapier;   rusty
He swoor by a' was swearing worth
    To speet him like a pliver,   plover
Unless he would from that time forth
    Relinquish her for ever.

Wi' ghastly e'e poor Tweedledee
    Upon his hunkers bended,   hams
An' pray'd for grace wi' ruefu' face,
    An' sae the quarrel ended.   so
But tho' his little heart did grieve
    When round the tinkler prest her,
He feign'd to snirtle in his sleeve   snigger
    When thus the caird address'd her:

SONG

TUNE: *Clout the Cauldron*   Patch

My bonie lass, I work in brass,
    A tinkler is my station;
I've travell'd round all Christian ground
    In this my occupation;
I've taen the gold, an' been enrolled
    In many a noble squadron;
But vain they search'd when off I march'd
    To go an' clout the cauldron.

Despise that shrimp, that wither'd imp,
    With a' his noise an' cap'rin,
An' take a share wi' those that bear
    The budget and the apron!
And by that stowp, my faith an' houpe!   pot
    And by that dear Kilbaigie!*
If e'er ye want, or meet wi' scant,   poverty
    May I ne'er weet my craigie!   wet; throat

* Whisky distilled at Kilbagie, Clackmannanshire.

RECITATIVO

The caird prevail'd: th' unblushing fair
  In his embraces sunk;
Partly wi' love o'ercome sae sair,
  An' partly she was drunk.
Sir Violino, with an air
    That show'd a man o' spunk,
Wish'd unison between the pair,
    An' made the bottle clunk
        To their health that night.

spirit

But hurchin Cupid shot a shaft,
    That play'd a dame a shavie:
The fiddler rak'd her fore and aft
    Behint the chicken cavie;
Her lord, a wight of Homer's craft,
    Tho' limpin' wi' the spavie,
He hirpl'd up, and lap like daft,
    An' shor'd them "Dainty Davie"
        O' boot that night.

urchin
trick
hencoop
spavin
hobbled; leapt
offered
as well

He was a care-defying blade
  As ever Bacchus listed!
Tho' Fortune sair upon him laid,
  His heart, she ever miss'd it.
He had no wish but – to be glad,
  Nor want but – when he thristed,
He hated nought but – to be sad;
  An' thus the Muse suggested
    His sang that night:

SONG

TUNE: *For A' That, An' A' That*

CHORUS

For a' that, an' a' that,
  An' twice as muckle's a' that,
I've lost but ane, I've twa behin',
  I've wife enough for a' that.

much

I am a Bard, of no regard
  Wi' gentle folks an' a' that,
But Homer-like the glowrin byke,
  Frae town to town I draw that.
    For a' that, &c.

staring crowd

I never drank the Muses' stank,   pond
    Castalia's burn, an' a' that;   brook
But there it streams, an' richly reams –   foams
    My Helicon I ca' that.
                For a' that, &c.

Great love I bear to a' the fair,
    Their humble slave an' a' that;
But lordly will, I hold it still
    A mortal sin to thraw that.   thwart
                For a' that, &c.

In raptures sweet, this hour we meet
    Wi' mutual love an' a' that;
But for how lang the flie may stang,   fly; sting
    Let inclination law that!
                For a' that, &c.

Their tricks an' craft hae put me daft,
    They've taen me in, an' a' that;
But clear your decks, an' here's the Sex!
    I like the jads for a' that.

CHORUS

For a' that, an' a' that,
    An' twice as muckle's a' that,
My dearest bluid, to do them guid,
    They're welcome till't for a' that!   to it

RECITATIVO

So sung the Bard, and Nansie's wa's   walls
Shook with a thunder of applause,
    Re-echo'd from each mouth!
They toom'd their pocks, they pawn'd their duds, emptied their ba
They scarcely left to coor their fuds,   cover; tails
    To quench their lowin drouth.   burning
Then owre again the jovial thrang   company
    The Poet did request
To lowse his pack, an' wale a sang,   untie; choose
    A ballad o' the best:
      He rising, rejoicing
        Between his twa Deborahs,
      Looks round him, an' found them
        Impatient for the chorus:

123

SONG

TUNE: *Jolly Mortals, Fill Your Glasses*

CHORUS

A fig for those by law protected!
Liberty's a glorious feast!
Courts for cowards were erected,
Churches built to please the priest!

I

See the smoking bowl before us!
Mark our jovial, ragged ring!
Round and round take up the chorus,
And in raptures let us sing:
A fig &c.

2

What is title, what is treasure,
What is reputation's care?
If we lead a life of pleasure,
'Tis no matter how or where!
A fig &c.

3

With the ready trick and fable
Round we wander all the day;
And at night in barn or stable
Hug our doxies on the hay.
A fig &c.

4

Does the train-attended carriage
Thro' the country lighter rove?
Does the sober bed of marriage
Witness brighter scenes of love?
A fig &c.

5

Life is all a variorum,
We regard not how it goes;
Let them prate about decorum,
Who have character to lose.
A fig &c.

Love and Liberty

6

Here's to budgets, bags and wallets!
　Here's to all the wandering train!
Here's our ragged brats and callets!
　One and all, cry out, Amen!
A fig &c.

THERE WAS A LAD

TUNE: *Dainty Davie*

CHORUS

Robin was a rovin boy,
Rantin, rovin, rantin, rovin,
Robin was a rovin boy,
Rantin, rovin Robin.

roistering

There was a lad was born in Kyle,
what   But whatna day o' whatna style,*
I doubt it's hardly worth the while
particular   To be sae nice wi' Robin.
Robin was &c.

one   Our monarch's hindmost year but ane
Was five-and-twenty days begun,
January wind   'Twas then a blast o' Janwar' win'
new-year gift   Blew hansel in on Robin.
Robin was &c.

glanced; palm   The gossip keekit in his loof,
Quoth she   Quo' scho: "Wha lives will see the proof,
thumping; dolt   This waly boy will be nae coof:
I think we'll ca' him Robin.
Robin was &c.

"He'll hae misfortunes great an' sma',
above   But ay a heart aboon them a'.
to   He'll be a credit till us a':
We'll a' be proud o' Robin!
Robin was &c.

"But sure as three times three mak nine,
every   I see by ilka score and line,
kind   This chap will dearly like our kin',
my blessings   So leeze me on thee, Robin!
Robin was &c.

make   "Guid faith," quo' scho, "I doubt you gar
aspread   The bonie lasses lie aspar;
faults; worse   But twenty fauts ye may hae waur –
So blessins on thee, Robin!"
Robin was &c.

---

* "on what day and by what method of dating". (The reformed calendar was adopted in Britain in 1751.)

AULD LANG SYNE

For auld lang syne, my dear,
  For auld lang syne,
We'll tak a cup o' kindness yet,
  For auld lang syne.

old long ago

Should auld acquaintance be forgot,
  And never brought to mind?
Should auld acquaintance be forgot,
  And auld lang syne?
                    For auld &c.

And surely ye'll be your pint-stowp!
  And surely I'll be mine!
And we'll tak a cup o' kindness yet,
  For auld lang syne.
                    For auld &c.

pay for

We twa hae run about the braes
  And pu'd the gowans fine;
But we've wander'd mony a weary foot
  Sin auld lang syne.
                    For auld &c.

hill-sides
pulled; wild daisies

since

We twa hae paidl'd i' the burn
  Frae mornin' sun till dine;
But seas between us braid hae roar'd
  Sin auld lang syne.
                    For auld &c.

waded; brook
noon
broad

And there's a hand, my trusty fiere!
  And gie's a hand o' thine!
And we'll tak a right gude-willy waught,
  For auld lang syne.
                    For auld &c.

comrade
give me
good-will drink

MY BONIE MARY

TUNE: *The Secret Kiss*

Go, fetch to me a pint o' wine,
  And fill it in a silver tassie,
That I may drink before I go
  A service to my bonie lassie!
The boat rocks at the pier o' Leith,
  Fu' loud the wind blaws frae the Ferry,
The ship rides by the Berwick-Law,
  And I maun leave my bonie Mary.

The trumpets sound, the banners fly,
  The glittering spears are rankèd ready,
The shouts o' war are heard afar,
  The battle closes deep and bloody.
It's not the roar o' sea or shore
  Wad mak me langer wish to tarry,
Nor shouts o' war that's heard afar:
  It's leaving thee, my bonie Mary!

must

AFTON WATER

Flow gently, sweet Afton, among thy green braes,   slopes
Flow gently, I'll sing thee a song in thy praise;
My Mary's asleep by thy murmuring stream,
Flow gently, sweet Afton, disturb not her dream!

Thou stock dove whose echo resounds thro' the
     glen,
Ye wild whistling blackbirds in yon thorny den,
Thou green-crested lapwing, thy screaming forbear —
I charge you, disturb not my slumbering Fair.

How lofty, sweet Afton, thy neighbouring hills,
Far mark'd with the courses of clear, winding rills;
There daily I wander, as noon rises high,
My flocks and my Mary's sweet cot in my eye.

How pleasant thy banks and green vallies below,
Where wild in the woodlands the primroses blow;
There oft, as mild ev'ning weeps over the lea,
The sweet-scented birk shades my Mary and me.   birch

Thy crystal stream, Afton, how lovely it glides,
And winds by the cot where my Mary resides!
How wanton thy waters her snowy feet lave,
As, gathering sweet flowerets, she stems thy clear
     wave.

Flow gently, sweet Afton, among thy green braes,
Flow gently, sweet river, the theme of my lays;
My Mary's asleep by thy murmuring stream,
Flow gently, sweet Afton, disturb not her dream.

WILLIE BREW'D A PECK O' MAUT

full (i.e. drunk)
droplet
crow; dawn
-brew

We are na fou, we're nae that fou,
But just a drappie in our e'e;
The cock may craw, the day may daw,
And ay we'll taste the barley-bree.

malt

live-long
would not have;
Christendom

O, Willie brewed a peck o' maut,
  And Rob and Allan cam to see.
Three blyther hearts that lee-lang night
  Ye wad na found in Christendie.
          We are na fou, &c.

more

Here are we met, three merry boys,
  Three merry boys I trow are we;
And monie a night we've merry been,
  And monie mae we hope to be!
          We are na fou, &c.

shining; sky; high
entice

It is the moon, I ken her horn,
  That's blinkin in the lift sae hie:
She shines sae bright to wyle us hame,
  But, by my sooth, she'll wait a wee!
          We are na fou, &c.

go
rogue

Wha first shall rise to gang awa,
  A cuckold, coward loun is he!
Wha first beside his chair shall fa',
  He is the king amang us three!
          We are na fou, &c.

AY WAUKIN, O

Ay waukin, O,   awake
   Waukin still and weary:
Sleep I can get nane
   For thinking on my dearie.

Simmer's a pleasant time:
   Flowers of every colour,
The water rins owre the heugh,   crag
   And I long for my true lover.
            Ay waukin, &c.

When I sleep I dream,
   When I wauk I'm eerie,   apprehensive
Sleep I can get nane
   For thinking on my dearie.
            Ay waukin, &c.

Lanely night comes on,
   A' the lave are sleepin: rest
I think on my bonie lad,
   And I bleer my een wi' greetin.   eyes; weeping
            Ay waukin, &c.

JOHN ANDERSON MY JO

John Anderson my jo, John,
   When we were first acquent,
Your locks were like the raven,
   Your bonie brow was brent;
But now your brow is beld, John,
   Your locks are like the snaw,
But blessings on your frosty pow,
   John Anderson my jo.

John Anderson my jo, John,
   We clamb the hill thegither,
And monie a cantie day, John,
   We've had wi' ane anither:
Now we maun totter down, John,
   And hand in hand we'll go,
And sleep thegither at the foot,
   John Anderson my jo.

acquainted (gloss for line 2)
smooth / *bald* (gloss)
pate (gloss)
climbed; together (gloss)
jolly (gloss)
must (gloss)

O, MERRY HAE I BEEN

TUNE: *Lord Breadalbane's March*

O, merry hae I been teethin a heckle,
   An' merry hae I been shapin a spoon:
O, merry hae I been cloutin a kettle,
   An' kissin my Katie when a' was done.
O, a' the lang day I ca' at my hammer,
   An' a' the lang day I whistle an' sing;
O, a' the lang night I cuddle my kimmer,
   An' a' the lang night as happy's a king.

Bitter in dool, I lickit my winnins
   O' marrying Bess, to gie her a slave.
Blest be the hour she cool'd in her linens,
   And blythe be the bird that sings on her grave!
Come to my arms, my Katie, my Katie,
   An' come to my arms, and kiss me again!
Drucken or sober, here's to thee, Katie,
   And blest be the day I did it again!

heckling-comb (gloss)
patching (gloss)
knock (gloss)
lass (gloss)
sorrow; supped; earnings* (gloss)
winding-sheet (gloss)

* i.e., made the best of a bad job.

THE BANKS O' DOON

TUNE: *Caledonian Hunt's Delight*

Ye banks and braes o' bonie Doon,   slopes
  How can ye bloom sae fresh and fair?
How can ye chant, ye little birds,
  And I sae weary fu' o' care!
Thou'll break my heart, thou warbling bird,
  That wantons thro' the flowering thorn:
Thou minds me o' departed joys,
  Departed never to return.

Aft hae I rov'd by bonie Doon
  To see the rose and woodbine twine,
And ilka bird sang o' its luve,   every
  And fondly sae did I o' mine.
Wi' lightsome heart I pu'd a rose,   plucked
  Fu' sweet upon its thorny tree;
And my fause luver staw my rose,   stole
  But ah! he left the thorn wi' me.

BONIE WEE THING

CHORUS

Bonie wee thing, cannie wee thing,   gentle
  Lovely wee thing, wert thou mine,
I wad wear thee in my bosom
  Lest my jewel it should tine.   lose

Wishfully I look and languish
  In that bonie face o' thine,
And my heart it stounds wi' anguish,   aches
  Lest my wee thing be na mine.
              Bonie wee &c.

Wit and Grace and Love and Beauty
  In ae constellation shine;   one
To adore thee is my duty,
  Goddess o' this soul o' mine!
              Bonie wee &c.

133

THE POSIE

O, luve will venture in where it daur na weel be
      seen,
O, luve will venture in, where wisdom ance hath
      been;
But I will doun yon river rove amang the wood sae
      green,
    And a' to pu' a posie to my ain dear May.

pluck

The primrose I will pu', the firstling o' the year,
And I will pu' the pink, the emblem o' my dear,
For she's the pink o' womankind, and blooms
      without a peer;
    And a' to be a posie to my ain dear May.

I'll pu' the budding rose when Phoebus peeps in
      view,

balmy

For it's like a baumy kiss o' her sweet, bonie mou.
The hyacinth's for constancy wi' its unchanging
      blue,
    And a' to be a posie to my ain dear May.

The lily it is pure, and the lily it is fair,
And in her lovely bosom I'll place the lily there.
The daisy's for simplicity and unaffected air,
    And a' to be a posie to my ain dear May.

The hawthorn I will pu', wi' its locks o' siller gray,
Where, like an agèd man, it stands at break o' day;

will not

But the songster's nest within the bush I winna tak
      away;
    And a' to be a posie to my ain dear May.

The woodbine I will pu' when the e'ening star is
      near,

eyes

And the diamond draps o' dew shall be her een sae
      clear;

claims

The violet's for modesty, which weel she fa's to
      wear,
    And a' to be a posie to my ain dear May.

I'll tie the posie round wi' the silken band o' luve
And I'll place it in her breast, and I'll swear by a'
    above,
That to my latest draught o' life the band shall ne'er
    remove,
    And this will be a posie to my ain dear May.

HEY, CA' THRO'

CHORUS

Hey, ca' thro', ca' thro',   work away
For we hae mickle ado,   much to do
Hey, ca' thro', ca' thro',
For we hae mickle ado.

Up wi' the carls of Dysart   old men
    And the lads o' Buckhaven,
And the kimmers o' Largo   gossips
    And the lasses o' Leven!
          Hey, ca' thro', &c.

We hae tales to tell,
    And we hae sangs to sing;
We hae pennies to spend,
    And we hae pints to bring.
          Hey, ca' thro', &c.

We'll live a' our days,
    And them that comes behin',
Let them do the like,
    And spend the gear they win!   wealth
          Hey, ca' thro', &c.

DUNCAN GRAY

1

Duncan Gray came here to woo,
    Ha, ha, the wooing o't,
On blythe Yule-Night when we were fou,
    Ha, ha, the wooing o't.
Maggie coost her head fu' high,
Look'd asklent and unco skeigh,
Gart poor Duncan stand abeigh;
    Ha, ha, the wooing o't.

Christmas Eve; drunk

cast
askance; very skittish
Made; off

2

Duncan fleech'd, and Duncan pray'd;
    Ha, ha, the wooing o't,
Meg was deaf as Ailsa Craig,
    Ha, ha, the wooing o't.
Duncan sigh'd baith out and in,
Grat his een baith bleer't an' blin',
Spak o' lowpin o'er a linn;
    Ha, ha, the wooing o't.

wheedled

both
Wept; eyes
leaping; waterfall

3

Time and Chance are but a tide,
    Ha, ha, the wooing o't,
Slighted love is sair to bide
    Ha, ha, the wooing o't.
"Shall I like a fool," quoth he,
"For a haughty hizzie die?
"She may gae to – France for me!"
    Ha, ha, the wooing o't.

hard to endure

jade
go

4

How it comes let doctors tell,
    Ha, ha, the wooing o't.
Meg grew sick, as he grew hale,
    Ha, ha, the wooing o't.
Something in her bosom wrings,
For relief a sigh she brings,
And O! her een they spak sic things!
    Ha, ha, the wooing o't.

such

5

Duncan was a lad o' grace,
  Ha, ha, the wooing o't,
Maggie's was a piteous case,
  Ha, ha, the wooing o't.
Duncan could na be her death,
Swelling pity smoor'd his wrath;   smothered
Now they're crouse and canty baith,   proud; jolly
  Ha, ha, the wooing o't.

OPEN THE DOOR TO
ME, O

TUNE: *Open the door softly*

O, open the door some pity to shew,
  If love it may na be, O:
Tho' thou hast been false, I'll ever prove true,
  O, open the door to me, O.

Cauld is the blast upon my pale cheek,
  But caulder thy love for me, O:
The frost, that freezes the life at my heart,
  Is nought to my pains frae thee, O.

The wan moon sets behind the white wave,
  And Time is setting with me, O:
False friends, false love, farewell! for mair
  I'll ne'er trouble them nor thee, O.

She has open'd the door, she has open'd it wide,
  She sees the pale corse on the plain, O:
"My true love!" she cried, and sank down by his
    side –
  Never to rise again, O.

O, WHISTLE AN' I'LL
COME TO YE, MY LAD

O, whistle an' I'll come to ye, my lad,
O, whistle an' I'll come to ye, my lad,
go   *Tho' father an' mother an' a' should gae mad,*
O, whistle an' I'll come to ye, my lad.

watch   But warily tent when ye come to court me,
not; -gate; ajar   And come nae unless the back-yett be a-jee;
Then   Syne up the back-style, and let naebody see,
not   And come as ye were na comin to me,
                        And come as ye were na comin to me.
                                      O, whistle &c.

                        At kirk, or at market, whene'er ye meet me,
Go; fly   Gang by me as tho' that ye car'd na a flie;
glance   But steal me a blink o' your bonie black e'e,
                        Yet look as ye were na lookin at me,
                        Yet look as ye were na lookin at me.
                                      O, whistle &c.

                        Ay vow and protest that ye care na for me,
sometimes; disparage;   And whyles ye may lightly my beauty a wee;
little   But court na anither, tho' jokin ye be,
                        For fear that she wyle your fancy frae me,
entice   For fear that she wyle your fancy frae me.
                                      O, whistle &c.

A RED, RED ROSE

TUNE: *Major Graham*

O my luve's like a red, red rose,
    That's newly sprung in June;
O my luve's like the melodie
    That's sweetly play'd in tune.

As fair art thou, my bonie lass,
    So deep in luve am I,
And I will luve thee still, my Dear,
    Till a' the seas gang dry.   go

Till a' the seas gang dry, my Dear,
    And the rocks melt wi' the sun:
I will luve thee still, my Dear,
    While the sands o' life shall run.

And fare thee weel, my only Luve,
    And fare thee weel a while!
And I will come again, my Luve,
    Tho' it were ten thousand mile!

CA' THE YOWES TO
THE KNOWES

CHORUS

Drive; ewes; knolls

brooklet runs

Ca' the yowes to the knowes,
Ca' them where the heather grows,
Ca' them where the burnie rowes,
   My bonie dearie.

thrush's

go

Hark, the mavis' e'ening sang
Sounding Clouden's woods amang,
Then a-faulding let us gang,
   My bonie dearie.
                Ca' the yowes &c.

We'll gae down by Clouden side,
Through the hazels, spreading wide
O'er the waves that sweetly glide
   To the moon sae clearly.
                Ca' the yowes &c.

Yonder Clouden's silent towers,
Where, at moonshine's midnight hours,
O'er the dewy bending flowers
   Fairies dance sae cheery.
                Ca' the yowes &c.

hobgoblin

Ghaist nor bogle shalt thou fear;
Thou'rt to Love and Heav'n sae dear
Nocht of ill may come thee near,
   My bonie dearie.
                Ca' the yowes &c.

Fair and lovely as thou art,
Thou hast stown my very heart;
I can die – but canna part,
   My bonie dearie.
                Ca' the yowes &.

FOR A' THAT AND A' THAT

Is there for honest poverty
   That hings his head, an' a' that?   hangs
The coward slave, we pass him by,
   We dare be poor for a' that!
For a' that, an' a' that,
   Our toils obscure, an' a' that,
The rank is but the guinea's stamp,
   The man's the gowd for a' that.   gold

What though on hamely fare we dine,
   Wear hoddin grey, an' a' that?   coarse grey woollen
Gie fools their silks, and knaves their wine,   cloth
   A man's a man for a' that.
For a' that, an' a' that,
   Their tinsel show, an' a' that,
The honest man, tho' e'er sae poor,
   Is king o' men for a' that.

Ye see yon birkie ca'd a lord,   fellow; called
   Wha struts, an' stares, an' a' that?
Tho' hundreds worship at his word,
   He's but a cuif for a' that.   dolt
For a' that, an' a' that,
   His ribband, star, an' a' that,
The man o' independent mind,
   He looks an' laughs at a' that.

A prince can mak a belted knight,
  A marquis, duke, an' a' that!
But an honest man's aboon his might –
  Guid faith, he mauna fa' that!
For a' that, an' a' that,
  Their dignities, an' a' that,
The pith o' sense an' pride o' worth
  Are higher rank than a' that.

Then let us pray that come it may
  As come it will for a' that,
That Sense and Worth o'er a' the earth
  Shall bear the gree an' a' that.
For a' that, an' a' that,
  It's comin yet for a' that,
That man to man the world o'er
  Shall brothers be for a' that.

Marginal glosses:
above
must not lay claim to

win; first place

O, WERT THOU IN THE CAULD BLAST

TUNE: *Lenox love to Blantyre*

O, wert thou in the cauld blast
　On yonder lea, on yonder lea,
My plaidie to the angry airt,　　　　　　　　　quarter
　I'd shelter thee, I'd shelter thee.
Or did misfortune's bitter storms
　Around thee blaw, around thee blaw,
Thy bield should be my bosom,　　　　　　　　shelter
　To share it a', to share it a'.

Or were I in the wildest waste,
　Sae black and bare, sae black and bare,
The desert were a paradise,
　If thou wert there, if thou wert there.
Or were I monarch o' the globe,
　Wi' thee to reign, wi' thee to reign,
The brightest jewel in my crown
　Wad be my queen, wad be my queen.

IT WAS A' FOR OUR
RIGHTFU' KING

TUNE: *Mally Stuart*

It was a' for our rightfu' king
  We left fair Scotland's strand;
It was a' for our rightfu' king,
    We e'er saw Irish land, my dear,
    We e'er saw Irish land.

Now a' is done that men can do,
  And a' is done in vain,
My Love and Native Land fareweel,
    For I maun cross the main, my dear,
    For I maun cross the main.

He turn'd him right and round about
  Upon the Irish shore,
And gae his bridle reins a shake,
    With adieu for evermore, my dear,
    And adieu for evermore!

The soger frae the wars returns,
  The sailor frae the main,
But I hae parted frae my love,
    Never to meet again, my dear,
    Never to meet again.

When day is gane, and night is come,
  And a' folk bound to sleep,
I think on him that's far awa
    The lee-lang night and weep, my dear,
    The lee-lang night and weep.

must

gave

live-long